Praise for *Customer 3D*

"Finally, a book that takes the customer experience to a new level. *Customer 3D* is a must read for any company, organization or individual that desires to set themselves apart. Bill captures the essence of being customer centric while providing a process and methodology to achieve excellence. The stories and examples Bill uses are excellent learning tools and make for a fascinating experience. Read it and implement it to reap the many benefits of *Customer 3D* including sustained increase in sales, deep customer loyalty and better overall satisfaction of employees and customers."

–Jim Ponder, President and CEO
Turnkey Strategic Relations

"There is a revolution under way in the business world. Self carefully lays out a holistic system that addresses ... a paradigm-busting plan for success."

–Kirkus Reviews

"*Customer 3D: A New Dimension for Customers* introduces new, important concepts that will be the catalyst for businesses to re-think their strategy. It replaces traditional, out-of-date practices with a vibrant system that will transform corporate cultures and deliver much higher organizational performance. This book expertly shows us the future and how companies will achieve powerful, expansive customer connections."

–Ken Potalivo, President
ProGrowth, Inc.

"*Customer 3D* deals with more than serving a customer. In this book you will discover how to transform your entire company into a customer-centric culture where all employees have the opportunity to provide solutions aimed at the customer. The book is non technical and will provide real answers that you can use in real time!"

–Jean Kelley, Author of *Look, Listen, Lead*
A Pocketbook Guide to Being a Memorable Leader

"*Customer 3D* is a book loaded with instantly applicable advice that can and will make you a better business person."

–**Larry Kilham**, founder of three companies and author of *MegaMinds: How to Create and Invent in the Age of Google*

"What does it truly mean to be customer-centric? *Customer 3D* challenges traditional thinking. In doing so, it forces you to look closely at the realities of your own organization - are you as customer-centered as you thought? Bill provides examples of customer-centricity, strategies to get there, and measurements to monitor progress. I recommend *Customer 3D* for any organization - to stimulate your thinking, re-energize your commitment to your customers, and define steps you can take."

–**Terry Callanan**, Chief Quality Officer
Carestream Health, Inc.

"Bill's extensive experience creating organizations to revolve around the customer provides a rich background in developing the deep change needed for extraordinary results. He goes beyond the typical rhetoric of customer service, providing specific, proven steps that drive passionate focus on your customer.
Customer 3D recognizes this transformation is hard work, but has enormous returns."

–**Robert Fetterman**, Vice President
Turning Stone Resort & Casino

"*Customer 3D* does exactly what the title says: It gives a whole new dimension to the art of customer service. With this more robust insight, owners, managers and entrepreneurs will be able to survive and thrive."

–**Pam Lontos**, President
Pam Lontos Consulting

"*Customer 3D* will help return the focus of a company's culture onto the customer, which is where it belongs. A must-read book for everyone in management."

–**John L Mariotti**, Award-winning co-author of *HOPE IS NOT A STRATEGY: Leadership Lessons from the Obama Presidency*

A new dimension
for customers

CUSTOMER 3D

Bill Self

Rochester, New York

CUSTOMER 3D™: A NEW DIMENSION FOR CUSTOMERS
By Bill Self
Copyright © 2012 Bill Self

Customer 3D is a trademark owned by CustomerEDU, LLC.

CustomerEDU
120 Allens Creek Road
Rochester, NY 14618
www.CustomerEDU.com
800-380-2308

ISBN 978-0-9853908-0-8 (paperback)

Book design and production by Heidi Wirth

Printed and bound in the United States of America

Dedicated to all organizations that believe the success of customers is the most important outcome of their work.

Acknowledgements

This book became possible because of the conversations, hard work, and shared insights of many dynamic individuals and important relationships. I must say Thank You for:

- The brilliant design thinking and balance provided by my colleague, Heidi Wirth, whose involvement was beyond the call of duty.
- The education about all things 3D from the expert, David Austin of AustinDesign3D.
- The support and counseling of my friend, Mark Frisk.
- The enabling efforts of my editor, Sandra Beckwith and the excellent proofreading diligence by Joy Hey Schnupp.
- The friendship and partnership of Nigel Hill, Jim Alexander and all of my colleagues at The Leadership Factor worldwide, who have consistently brought new ideas and excellence to the design of better customer measurement systems.
- Most of all, the organizations whose stories are inside this book, who have generously shared their leadership and culture development ideas in order to help other companies benefit.

The Customer 3D movement has already started because of many dedicated and thoughtful people who believe that there is a new dimension of performance for customers that more companies need to expand into.

Introduction

Exceptional.

In every aspect of our lives, we encounter extraordinary people and organizations, and we all want to know how they do it. So we follow their stories, hoping to figure out the secrets that make them so successful.

Throughout my career in customer research, I have been fascinated by how organizations in the top 2 percent in customer relations outperform all the others. They're consistently ranked at the top of their industry sectors and of businesses collectively; they are rewarded with top-box satisfaction and loyalty levels from their customers.

But why are they so much better than the overwhelming majority of companies? It's not that the average performers don't care about their customers – most of them do! Instead, as I've discovered, the average performers simply don't know how to create a new dimension of customer satisfaction. They're locked into a product-centered approach to customers because they don't understand that to be successful, they must become customer-centric. This book will change that.

If organizations are going to perform better for their customers, they must abandon the business-as-usual structure where leaders hope that linear progress along a product-centric journey will create more loyal customers. That is painfully slow and too disjointed. And, frankly, because it is relatively easy to copy products, the loyalty that product-centric companies generate is temporary. Customer-centricity, on the other hand, creates permanent relationships.

Most customer relationship models are flat and one-dimensional (1D) because traditional approaches are transaction-driven and product-centric. But there is a new model, one that is deeper, stronger and more fully developed. It is three-dimensional (3D), organic, and customer-centric. Companies using this model place the customer at the center of their purpose and build a corresponding 3D culture within by focusing on solutions for the customer.

These high-performing 3D organizations are beginning to change the course of global business by creating a movement that is gaining momentum. They realize that customer-centricity is not achieved by controlling individual transactions; it happens by creating a system that makes it possible for employees to perform at their highest level on every transaction. Until now, we haven't had a name for this system. Now we can call it Customer 3D.

This Customer 3D system used by top performers incorporates a customer strategy based on working for the customer, not the company or its product line. These extraordinary organizations are at the top because they know that being customer-centered makes them the best they can be. They don't focus on their products and then care about customers as an after-thought. The best performers in entertainment and sports sell tickets by giving the audience their all. The same is true in business. When there's a top-quality performance, success follows. It's about how you connect with the audience – your customers – to make their outcomes more valuable and memorable.

Contrast that with an organization with strategies that involve nothing more than products and financials. The lack of a customer strategy means employees are left on their own to do their best with customers. There's no leadership or consistency throughout the organization, so results are lackluster at best. And yet, most organizations operate this way.

This "sameness" creates another problem, too – a lack of differentiation. It's difficult for customers to see what makes one of these companies different from or better than its competitors. Customers might, in fact, describe one of these businesses by saying, "They make the same product as their competitors." 3D companies, on the other hand, are never seen as commodity providers. They are viewed as leaders, the organizations setting the standard for others to be compared against. As customers, we don't always fully understand the success of these high-performers. We say, "They have good people," without recognizing that they have a good system that develops these good people.

VIII Because of that system, employees in 3D organizations never have a bad day at work. They are customer-focused and believe that what they are doing matters. They have an emotional connection to the company's customer-focused goals and they understand the need to be more consultative with customers. They love taking responsibility for the customer and being empowered to deliver ideas that are fresh and creative. And they respect customers' intelligence, which is why they joined the company in the first place.

A System for Originality

I wrote this book to provide organizations with a system that will transform their cultures. Most traditional companies have perfected the management models of the 1990s. The mix of systems these companies use to serve customers are all edging closer to becoming obsolete because they are product-centered. Clearly, thanks to technology, all organizations are faster in their response to customers than in the past. But they will continue to lose ground to the exceptional performers because they are seen as one-dimensional. In fact, with the exception of technology that allows companies to automate and accelerate processes that used to be manual, it's difficult to identify any new customer systems today that differ from the traditional. Customer 3D changes all of that. It creates originality. With a customer-centered strategy, success is not transitory because it permeates everything the organization delivers.

While many companies say (and even *believe*) they care for the customer, it's mostly just lip service. That's why this book is so important. It doesn't dust off platitudes that have been around for years. It's not a "back-to-basics approach" that says we have lost our way on a journey that used to be customer-focused. Rather, it offers a new definition of prosperity built off of higher-level concepts about how to achieve unprecedented performance in a dimension that has been under-developed until now. It is a fundamental shift, not in outcomes or goals, but in the path taken to accomplish those goals.

The purpose of the Customer3D system is to transform organizations that are looking for a fresher, more productive system. It shows them the techniques for becoming customer-centered, which means thinking like their customers. The Customer 3D approach delivers an organization that has both strength and balance. It generates a longevity that is built on a foundation of customer closeness.

The customer-centered champions in this book didn't arrive at that status haphazardly. They have created a wholeness that is recognizable (even if subconsciously) by customers. These organizations are more alive and more intense than the others in their industries. They are led by a culture (yes, a *culture*, not a *CEO!*) committed to changing "how we look to our customers." An organizational design that delivers a more fully developed connection to customers motivates these efforts. It leads to fully engaged employees who operate with few limitations when it comes to making customers feel closer and more committed to the organization.

The classic view of customer relations talks about satisfaction, loyalty, recommending, re-purchase and the usual elements that most product-centric organizations believe are the be-all and the end-all. We have developed a new "classic," though, that delivers and sustains even higher performance for businesses. Customer 3D is a dynamic approach that will create a highly customer-centered organization – one that is both elegant and effective in what it does. Customer 3D organizations have richer, more beautiful, and more human relationships with their customers. They are originals – because they have developed authentic customer relationships that no one can match. While products can be replicated, a customer-centric culture can't be copied by the competition. That's a big payback for 3D organizations.

Customer-Centering

Customer 3D is a flexible system of leadership focused on developing and sustaining a culture in which customers are at the center of every activity. It works for all companies, large or small. Copernicus was ridiculed for saying the Earth was not the center of the solar system (and the universe as it was known at that time). We know today that our organizations are not the center of the universe, which is why it's hard to understand why many companies still operate that way. The best way to break out of that company-centered 1D paradigm into 3D is to understand that new ideas and solutions must be centered on customers.

Breakthrough 3D companies develop self-organizing systems that act as the organization's central nervous system. This, in turn, acts on behalf of the customer. These businesses work from a customer-directed set of goals and a fully understood customer strategy. Companies that don't understand that customers are at the center of their purpose are simply operating in a product-centric world where their best hope is for pleasant customer encounters. 3D organizations have a customer-focused purpose that drives all actions inside the company. Whether they want to help their customers become healthier or enjoy financial security, they put their customers' best interests first.

Companies that are really, really customer-centered separate themselves from their competition because they do a few key things very well and they do them systematically. Customer 3D is a model to better understand the reasons for doing so. It shows how re-orienting the approach will make organizations prosper to a degree that they didn't think was possible. It's a model of innovation and corporate culture designed around and for the customer. It is a re-orientation and a culture change that will expand the way that your organization will perform.

3D companies are exceptional because they have a purpose defined by customer success. This is always expanding into more logical, productive, and creative performances. The end result is a much closer relationship with customers. 3D companies are not traditional organizations trying to make cosmetic changes. Rather, they design and grow powerful cultures that are focused on making history. You will never be more than average if you don't take this approach. If you want to be an exceptional performer for your customers, it's time to take your culture to a new dimension.

Contents

PART 1

Do You Want to Know a Secret?: How Being Customer-Centered Creates the 3D Organization

*Companies… don't just create; they execute
and compete and coordinate the efforts
of many different people, and the organizations
that are most successful at that task are the
ones where the system is the star.*
Malcolm Gladwell, What the Dog Saw

Successful organizations believe that all change has an impact on customers or comes from customers. That philosophy drives how they see their world; they build their story from that foundation. Customer-centered organizations don't walk down paths created by others – they create new paths that take them to what's important to them.

Customer 3D companies share that journey with their customers while, at the same time, they understand that it's the customer's journey, not the company's, that matters. Their sense of direction rises out of a customer-centric culture. They are driven by outcomes hat define success for their customers – health, convenience, happiness, beauty, high quality, vitality – depending on the markets they serve. For them, products are secondary to customer relationships.

Their business model based on customer purpose – being customer-centered – is much stronger, more effective, and solid than product centering. It creates richer, more robust relationships with customers

I

that are, quite frankly, more real. That is why they are 3D.

The term "customer-centric" has been kidnapped by many organizations that use it to describe business-as-usual customer service. Renaming behaviors, though, doesn't change (or improve) them. In this book, what we call "customer-centric" behavior takes companies on a new trajectory – beyond product-centric. This different centering on an external purpose – in this case, using added value to create a better life for the customer – generates new energy and exciting ideas.

When we work with companies to improve their customer service, we start by asking executives how customers describe them today, but also how they want customers to describe them in two or three years. We get interesting answers; most tend to be fairly traditional. We help them see that the journey from product-centered to customer-centered produces entirely different words, some of which are more substantive and far-reaching. The traditional words are not wrong, of course, but the mindset they engender can be limiting. The vibrant 3D companies featured in this book, on the other hand, use words and phrases that are much bolder. They include:

- Freedom to act
- Sense of purpose
- Proactive
- Family-like
- Responsive
- Empowering
- Strong

Yoga teaches students to begin from their foundation – their heart and feet. In business, organizations that believe that being value-driven will deliver success also believe that the customer is their foundation. They understand that their performance can't move beyond ordinary to extraordinary without a culture that empowers employees to think like their customers.

ONE

How to ID (Identify) 3D

Your work is going to fill a large part of your life,
and the only way to be truly satisfied
is to do what you believe is great work.
And the only way to do great work
is to love what you do.
Steve Jobs, 2005 Commencement Address, Stanford University

Organizations don't realize that they're under-performing for customers. They're shackled by a belief that the one-dimensional (1D) approach they have been taught is all that's needed – in fact, they believe it's all that's available. 1D organizations say, "The customer is important." Three-dimensional (3D) organizations say, "The success (and lifestyle and prosperity) of the customer is important." And 3D companies have a system and culture that delivers this vision. That system is what we call "Customer 3D."

Customer 3D organizations are originals. They have a clear concept of their 3D approach, defining (with flexibility) their role in the customer's success and making it coherent to employees. When the message is communicated well throughout the organization, it adds a life and agility that delivers unmatched performance to the organization's customers. 3D companies believe their customers are smart and, rather than treating them condescendingly, they want to think like them. Everything employees do supports this concept without compromise.

3

Why Call It 3D?

Customer 3D is more complete and substantive than simple transactional customer service, which is one-dimensional. Because it's proactive, it's a powerful and sustainable game-changer for companies that commit to making the journey into this positive dimension.

The addition of proactive, customer-centric systems transforms businesses into more fully developed, complete, and vital organizations – they become Customer 3D. In contrast, one-dimensional organizations appear shallow and flat. Customers perceive these operations as less human because they are mechanical, treating them with indifference. These organizations claim to care about customers, but they aren't customer-focused. The company, not the customer, comes first.

1D organizations operate from a philosophy of what feels like scarcity – they believe that there are limited ideas out there, so they guard theirs from competitors and customers. Customers don't accept this approach anymore, though. They see it as deficient – as a system that no longer delivers trust to customers in the way it once did. Product-centricity led us to this deficiency; customer-centricity will help us find the way through it.

If 1D is exemplified by sluggishness, 3D, at the other end of the spectrum, enjoys a high energy level that is focused on continuous improvements for the customer. Customer 3D is more substantive than 1D, which is manifested in transactional customer service. Because 3D is proactive, it's a powerful and sustainable game-changer for companies that commit to making the journey. Because 3D is more visual (it comes from design and creativity more than engineering and control), organizations practicing it can better visualize success moving forward.

The 3D approach requires that every activity, change, policy and approach move the organization toward being customer-centered. It's transformative, and while "regular" change stands alone, transformative change permeates the entire organization. The 3D approach teaches managerial savvy instead of pushing the organization to follow an inflexible formula. Because 3D organizations encourage freedom in their cultures, they enjoy many more exciting, energizing activities that are contagious and empower even more positive change. Essentially, Customer 3D organizations make more sense to their customers and employees. Interactions in 1D companies, on the other hand, are burdensome for customers, employees and management.

Self Portrait

All organizations should have a clean, clear vision of how they look to their customers. Their 3D vision includes every aspect of the relationship, from product quality and

> You were born an original.
> Don't die a copy.
> *John Mason*

transactional courtesy to how focused the culture is on customer success. Customer 3D is a lens that enables a new way to see the organization and, at the same time, a new way to be seen by customers.

3D is about realism. The Customer 3D view begins with the belief that the relationship between a supplier and its customers is worth more than one sale. It is this solid foundation that allows companies to stretch beyond one-dimensional – in a calm, natural, almost effortless way – by practicing a no-limitations philosophy for

5

customers. The Customer 3D approach expands organizations to a dimension that is both alive and original.

If you choose to rise above product-centricity, you have to emphasize, accentuate, and feature customers by placing them at the center of everything your organization does. The message should not be simply to highlight the customer, but to make certain that everything your company does keeps the customer perspective in mind. It should expand the organization by embracing the reality that customers are your reason for existing. Doing this creates a vitality that is truly three-dimensional.

Barlean's Label-on-Label

Customer 3D requires the ability to think like a customer; thinking like a customer requires an unselfish approach to business. An excellent example of a 3D company with an unselfish business model is Barlean's Organic Oils of Ferndale, Wash. CIO Jade Beutler says the company focuses on "making things intuitive for consumers." Founded in 1989, the seller of organic nutritional products that include fish oils and flax seed is driven by the fact that eight out of 10 Americans are deficient in essential fats. Knowing that this deficiency can lead to a variety of diseases and health problems, company employees focus on their customers' health and see their efforts as, Beutler says, "a pleasure, not a chore." As part of its commitment to offering the freshest products, for example, Barlean's proactively began stamping a six-month freshness date on labels even though competitors use the allowable one-year range. The message to consumers? Barlean's delivers a fresher product.

I became familiar with Barlean's as one of its customers. I didn't notice anything special until I encountered a new label on its Forti-Flax product. The company used a unique and incredibly effective approach: it placed the old label on top of the new one. The label read, "To Reveal Barlean's New Look...Peel." Customers like me recognized the "old" label on the shelf – but also got a preview of the "new" label we'd see the next time we shopped for our favorite Barlean's products.

This told me I was buying from a truly innovative, customer-caring company. When transitioning to the new label, the people at

Barlean's put themselves in the customers' shoes before developing the "peel here" concept. As a result, the customer saw what he was looking for on the shelf, enjoyed peeling off the "old" label to reveal the new version (like opening a present), and then put the new label on the shelf at home. When it was time to buy more, the product had a now-recognizable label which would be easy to identify at the store.

A product-centric company would have simply replaced the older label. Barlean's, however, chose to use a more expensive – but more effective – approach to help customers become familiar with the new look. Barlean's management intrinsically understands that taking these customer-friendly actions will create more loyalty and brand strength – all of which supports continued growth. In an age of product sameness, thinking like a customer at every possible touch point helps capture the customer's mindshare.

Another example of Barlean's 3D approach to customer service is its Omega Swirl product. This innovative creation makes the company's fish and flax oil supplements more palatable by adding a compound that eliminates the oily texture. The result, with the taste and texture of a fruit smoothie, makes the healthy product much more appealing. Developed in response to customers' requests for a less fishy-tasting product, it won *Better Nutrition Magazine*'s award for best new supplement product in 2008.

In addition, there's no minimum order requirement and a no-questions-asked return policy. The company believes that the competition is not the enemy, an attitude that contributes to its goal of building the organic food products segment into an industry category. With an outstanding staff and an unadulterated approach to thinking like a customer, Barlean's is sure to succeed by continuing to differentiate itself. With the philosophy, "How are we going to delight our customer?" Barlean's is truly 3D.

Recognizing 3D

Barlean's label-on-label concept is one of hundreds of creative improvements the company is making for its customers. Its culture supports this type of unselfish concern for customers to the point that every action employees take is done *for* their customers, not *to* them.

7

As Barlean's has shown, 3D has its own identity, recognizable no matter who is delivering it. The 3D organization attracts customers because of positive qualities that include:

- A purpose outside the four walls of the organization
- An attitude that extends beyond a sales mindset so that a customer purchase is secondary to the outcomes that the customers receive and value
- Cohesion and coherence, with no mixed messages to customers or employees
- A lack of self-importance or arrogance
- A solid understanding of what the organization is and what it wants to accomplish for customers (and it does a great job of communicating this to employees)
- The ability to act as a bridge to customers resulting in stronger relationships
- Being able to provide expanded customer experiences that go beyond the ordinary encounters that customers consider to be average and expected

Most customer relationship strategies are one-dimensional. But the new 3D model – one that is deeper, stronger and more fully developed – places the customer at the center of a company's purpose. It creates a 3D culture that attracts and keeps customers because the organization and its employees think like those customers. Customer 3D is a philosophy and management style that allows companies to be the most customer-centered in their industries.

What Does 1D Look Like?

What has changed in dealing with customers in the last two decades? Other than technology, not much. And that is precisely the problem. 1D companies believe that technology offers the future – it's business as usual, only faster. But, autopilot, which is tempting because it's comfortable, is dangerous in any business.

One-dimensional organizations are shallow. They are concerned only with themselves and their products. Most of these organizations feel pressure from competitors trying to turn their products into commodities, which lowers their pricing. 3D companies, on the other hand, literally work in a different dimension. Rather than worrying

8

about competitors, they focus on high-quality products and service because of the close relationship with their customers.

How can you tell if a company is *not* customer-centric? If you feel compelled to talk to someone's supervisor, you know that the company's training and empowerment hasn't gone deep enough. If you find the company indifferent to customers, you know that employees are not purposeful. If you encounter many rules and procedures, you know that the organization is product-centric, not customer-centric.

Empowering Employees

When I asked Julie Auslander, president and chief cultural officer of cSubs, how she wanted customers to describe her company, she used language like resourceful, energetic, easy-to-work-with, flexible, nimble, and seamless. She listed them in one breath, without hesitation. Auslander's goal is to make this vision a reality by focusing the entire organization on the success of its customers.

cSubs, an award-winning business, helps clients save time and money on subscriptions, books, memberships, software licenses, and other products that must be periodically renewed. By managing periodical subscriptions and services through the company's website, cSubs' clients ensure that all of their account activity is centralized on a single invoice. The company has combined innovation and passion for customer success to gain the trust and loyalty of hundreds of businesses. Clients include many of the world's largest corporations because cSub's professionalism, customized programs, and service are unmatched in the industry.

Auslander envisions – and delivers – a company that produces a high-quality customer experience grounded in total team engagement. The company's culture is built on servant leadership philosophies developed by Robert Greenleaf and others. Employees are trained to understand that customer relationships are their most important responsibility.

"We are far less concerned with the individual transaction than with the customer relationship," Auslander says.

Company leaders empower employees by providing encouragement

9

and resources that make great customer service possible. While employees must follow a series of tested problem-solving steps before deviating from the norm to help customers, there are no rigid rules. Even so, employees understand that they will have to "go outside the box" almost every day – and they have the authority to do so to create happy customers.

David Rifkin, the company's executive vice president, emphasizes the importance of building and maintaining cordial relationships with customers. He tells employees, "We want your phone manner to be such that we can't tell whether you're talking with your sister or your customer."

The culture building process asks employees to share problems they've had with other companies – maybe they couldn't find a sales person in a store, or the sales person wouldn't leave the department to help find an item. They talk about making sure people don't have those complaints about cSubs. Rifkin believes this helps the company avoid providing weak customer service by reminding employees what it's like to be on the receiving end when interacting with customers.

(Don't) Paint by the Numbers

Some of you might remember the paint-by-numbers kits that were popular in the mid-20th Century because they gave users the false perception that they were creating "art." In reality, "painters" were creating a weak imitation. Many 1D businesses mimic this model when managing customer service programs. It doesn't work. To be truly 3D, organizations allow their employees' creativity to surface in order to allow their customer-centered "masterpiece" to emerge. Don't expect customer loyalty to appear because you have followed a formulaic approach. Creative beats formulaic every time.

All leaders should be skeptical of any proposal to manage customer connections based on lists from a book – even this one. Lists are too prescriptive, too non-customer-centric. Instead, go back to your customers' basic needs and work forward from that point. Produce intelligence that leads to meaningful answers about how the customer will prosper. Ask, "How will our customers be better?" when your organization succeeds. This is the essence of a customer-centric culture. If you are going to paint a masterpiece, it won't be by following the numbers. It will be because you've garnered the collective passion that exists within your organization. When your talents are directed toward thinking like a customer, your customer connections will rise to a level that others envy.

Picturing the Difference

As the fishbone diagram in Figure 1.1 illustrates, a 1D company's goal is to sell products. The diagram highlights the way 1D companies put their emphasis on how customers will buy and use their products or services. They view their customer needs as the same – to use the products they produce. They secure customers only because customers mean sales and profits. 1D companies like this have trouble recognizing and helping those customers that need flexibility. The customer is inevitably swallowed up in the product-centric machine because the organization exists only to make and sell more products. 3D organizations, on the other hand, emphasize optimizing performance and quality for customers. The customer is the catalyst behind every decision.

That product-centered business engages in a monologue with customers. 1D organizations are indifferent toward customers because customer satisfaction isn't the primary goal – the primary goal is selling products. Customers are replaceable. They don't mean that much to the organization except in terms of sales revenue.

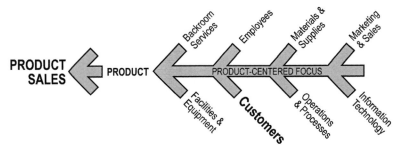

Figure 1.1

Contrast the product-centric focus with the customer-centered approach in Figure 1.2. Organizationally, nothing has changed. However, the focus is on customer success, not product sales. Products are still involved, of course, but the role of these products is

II

to make customers' lives better, easier, healthier, more efficient, and more enjoyable. The organization's purpose is helping customers achieve success and products are simply part of the balance.

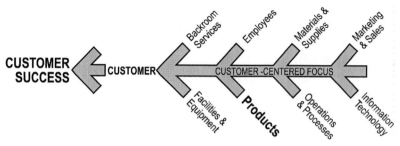

Figure 1.2

Re-Prioritizing the Organization

When you imagine the fishbone diagrams together as a two-sided jigsaw puzzle metaphor, it's easy to see that all of the pieces are the same, but assembled in a more dynamic way that benefits the customer. This helps take some of the fear out of the process of transforming a company into one that is customer-centered. You don't necessarily have to do things differently – it's more a matter of re-prioritizing the things that are already being done so that you emphasize the components that will make the organization more customer-driven. Although the same pieces are involved, the customer-centered version is stronger and more sustainable.

The beauty of this is that this attitude adjustment taps into a nascent spirit in the culture. As the organization enjoys successes that are communicated to employees, the organization's spirit rises even further in a spiral effect. There's more abundance and less scarcity.

In contrast, 1D companies are notoriously insular, which leads to territorial business decisions based on controlling, narrow sets of priorities. These misguided strategies don't consider customers because managers mistakenly rationalize that "we've got more important things to do." It's confusing and frustrating to customers when organizations operate in 1D, rather than in 3D. Now, more than ever, businesses are moving toward Customer 3D to create the right set of priorities that will focus their decisions on what is important and valuable to their customers.

12

Short-Term Thinking

Those priorities don't include short-term thinking, which has plagued businesses for years. In today's economic environment, though, it is even more dangerous. Now is the time for change. Rather than retreating into survival mode, forward-thinking organizations are focusing on identifying customer needs and gathering the energy of the entire business to find solutions for these opportunities. The best way to identify these emerging customer needs is by thinking like a customer. Adopting a 3D approach to organizational culture will position progressive companies for the future. It becomes a fundamental "reset" that will change the way your organization does business forever.

1D organization leaders must realize that they can't recycle past ideas and hope to live off of an old reputation. They might not admit that customer change is happening, but it's there. Like watching a ship move almost imperceptibly on the ocean, we don't realize until minutes later that it has, indeed, moved dramatically.

Six Sigma and other efforts at internal efficiencies have run their course largely because they concentrated on constricting existing processes. Frankly, many of these efficiencies were never noticed by customers. The new way – Customer 3D – is expansive. The gauge for evaluating improvements going forward will be how changes impact customers. Thinking like a customer during today's difficult times will lock in customer loyalty that will sustain growth for years to come. Doing more – and doing it now – not only applies to internal excellence, but to improvements that will impact customers, too.

"Tells"

"Tells" are indicators of what others see in you – how you behave in any situation. Customers use all of your interactions with them – your "tells" – to form an impression of how you will treat them in the future. It's important to understand these tells and to manage them deliberately.

A tell in poker is a subtle but noticeable change in a player's behavior or demeanor that gives you a sense of what that player thinks of his hand of cards. A tell in business is any organizational interaction – human or technological – that indicates how you *really* operate. Customers will pick up on them very quickly. If a tell is negative, it will send a direct message that you don't want them as customers.

Every company has thousands of tells that communicate to customers what its culture is like. The important thing to realize is that these tells must be managed across the entire organization – not transactionally with good "service" from front-line employees – but strategically company-wide. The structure must be recursive, built on customer-centered procedures or approaches that can be applied repeatedly. Success will be related to strong feedback loops that keep the business in touch with its customers.

Here's an example. When I travel, I use one hotel chain more than 90 percent of the time. I'm in the top 5 percent of the company's customers, claiming elite status in its rewards program. The company knows a lot about my preferences and habits. Yet, until recently, every time I reserved a room online, the system asked me for my AAA (American Automobile Association) number. Don't you think they could save that information in my account? Why should I have to pull the card from my wallet and enter the number every time?

I find it hard to believe that no employee has experienced this process as a company customer and not questioned it. When I asked about it, a rewards help desk employee said that other customers have made the request, too, but he couldn't do anything about it. Since it seemed to be my responsibility – rather than the help desk employee's – to push for a change, I made the suggestion through an online feedback option. I got a response – but it wasn't what I expected. I learned that the company's reservation template doesn't have enough fields to store these numbers in files. Clearly, the constraints of the hotel's computer system were more important than the inconveniences to its customers.

I wonder how that help desk employee would rate his employer on its willingness to fix a problem. My firm has many clients that proactively ask their customers to do exactly that – to rate them not on how they have addressed a specific problem, but to comment on whether they have faith that the organization will take ownership

14

of a future problem. If you are customer-focused, you want to score high on this question because it announces whether your customers trust you to provide value. Do you know and measure this critical assessment with your customers? (See Chapter 7 for information on how to do this.)

When building a customer-centric business, the first objective is to eliminate all negative tells. This requires a philosophy of reciprocity where both sides are working on the other's behalf in the exchange. Tells will give you away if they are negative, but will reinforce your stature if they are positive.

Companies don't forget their customers – they simply take them for granted. You can't hide this offhanded attitude for long because of the tells. On your journey to becoming customer-centered, look at every tell and make certain that it plainly shows that your organization is thinking like a customer.

Arrogance Isn't Allowed

There is a common paradox among many companies as they become more successful: they tend to become removed from the customers who have contributed to their success. 1D companies can also be undermined by their own success when they become arrogant or believe they are invincible. The Achilles heel of successful organizations is the feeling that their success will never end. Going forward, they attempt to sustain these successes by repeating product-centric tactics that worked in the past. However, what got them there has a shelf life, a saturation point. When there's a decline, it's usually because the product suffers from neglect or the company fails to recognize the fundamental importance of its relationships with customers.

In the 21st Century, one thing is certain: success runs aren't long unless customers are deeply involved. When organizations lose their edge, it infiltrates the rank and file. The antidote to overcoming this negativism is an unmitigated commitment to one goal: Creating customer success and loyalty. Customer 3D introduces a customer-centered mentality that is clearly cultural and grounded in values. It uses processes that become self-reinforcing.

15

The ultimate way to stay on top is through strength in performance for customers. 3D winners focus on how they can keep their lead – not in a selfish way, but through abundance. Embrace the philosophy, "Give and you shall later get." This results in organizational self-confidence, greater adaptability, huge leaps in resourcefulness, and an open attitude toward new ideas.

> Success is a lousy teacher. It seduces smart people into thinking they can't lose.
> *Bill Gates*

When people have confidence in each other, energy frees up because the organization trusts that everyone is acting in the best interest of the customer. People begin to respect each other and when they feel respected, they don't want to disappoint teammates. They will do just about anything to outperform. Peer pressure is a wonderful thing, sending a message that everyone in the organization can make a difference.

This generates successful customer experiences, which in turn builds the confidence needed to continue to get better. The essential premise is that your individual or corporate performance means nothing unless your customers value it – and it spreads because it empowers employees to grow in their relationships with your customers. 3D organizations know that putting the customer at the heart of your business will galvanize the efforts of the entire team. You're all working for the same thing, right?

There is a very humble, but confident attitude that is shared by all 3D organizations. They think the system they have developed is simple and they wonder why other companies haven't adopted it. The reason, of course, is that those other businesses see their performance through a product lens. 3D companies, instead, think like their customers. Emphasizing customer-centricity should be the foundation of every successful future. How you create and sustain the confidence that exudes from a winning streak is the same as how you get the best out of your organization – through unwavering customer focus.

Customer Effort

The Customer 3D system helps organizations focus on understanding how much effort a customer must exert to do business with them.

16

The objective, of course, is to minimize this effort – not by asking customers how much effort they had to put forth, but by internally evaluating every process to make these interactions easier and less time-consuming for those customers.

Smart business people tackle these "effort" challenges for customers proactively. They don't need to ask customers how much effort was required – they already know. After all, they created the system the customer is using. A good measure of an organization's focus on customer success is how customers perceive their "return on effort." In other words, what value is the business providing compared to competitors? High-performing companies are always searching for ways to design more user-friendly processes that are more intuitive for their customers. That should be the top priority every day because it will pay off with happier, more loyal customers in the long-term. Reducing customer effort can best be achieved in a "question-everything" organizational culture. Don't wait for the customer to ask about it or give you a low score on a satisfaction survey.

As online purchases become more commonplace, all forms of customer experiences – both personal and "self-service" – have to be understood and rigorously questioned. If you want to improve systems, approach customer touch points with a design mindset and you'll find a number of possible improvements.

Truly customer-centered companies are always looking more broadly than their narrow business model to discover innovative ways to make life, in general, easier for their customers, even if those solutions are above-and-beyond the products and services that they sell.

Customers Who Tolerate Us

My bank has a no-better-than-adequate online banking system. The employees know it. They hear it all the time from customers and they put up with it themselves. I recently spoke with one employee who told me that:

- The bank spent a lot of money to develop the system and doesn't want to spend more (or admit it made a mistake).
- Customers tolerate it. They don't seem to complain enough to warrant a change.

You can't convince me that its leaders think it's great or even above average. Fortunately, the front-line employees at this bank are fantastic. However, if these employees understand how irritating the online banking system is, why don't the executives? Are they using their own system for financial transactions? If the investment in the computer system was hefty, it is undoubtedly embarrassing to admit the mistake and invest more. But, it needs to be done to stay competitive.

"Because customers tolerate it" is no longer an acceptable excuse in any forward-thinking organization. It's a 1D approach that will not create champion organizations. Every dynamic company that cares about its customers must have a system that helps it discover customer frustrations and develop solutions. You will learn how to do this in Parts II and III. It's one thing to talk about customer care; it's another thing to share the journey with customers by providing what they need and expect.

What would a 3D organization do? It would create a project team to re-design the online banking system by:

- Identifying customer needs and current system shortfalls
- Announcing the project in advance to employees and ask for input about the improvements that they know customers want to see
- Comparing state-of-the-art online systems at other banks, then innovating to exceed offerings from those systems

Customer 3D will demonstrate how to design organizations that customers love to work with, rather than simply tolerate. The closer that a business puts customers at the center of its strategy, the more weight it will carry with those customers and the stronger the gravitational pull that it will generate.

Making Sense

Customers struggle to "make sense" of 1D product-centric companies. 3D companies with systems that make sense to smarter, more experienced customers have a corporate culture with a clear, shared vision that unifies efforts into a whole. That "whole" then connects with customers and makes sense to them.

Customer-centered organizations evaluate their performance based on what their customers think. The mission of WD-40 Company, Inc., for instance, is to create positive lasting memories for its customers. WD-40 is a global consumer products company; its lubricants and cleaners are found under the sink, in the garage and in toolboxes of loyal fans in more than 160 countries.

To define its focus, the company concentrates on consumers. Its philosophy is that "100 percent of our business comes from our end-users. They are our ultimate customer. Without them we are nothing," comments CEO Garry Ridge. "Our ideas don't matter," he adds. The company wants to improve customers' memories of their experiences with WD-40 products – how they felt afterward – to drive product innovation. It's about sharing the experience with the customer, not imposing company processes on that experience.

In the 1970's, "adhocracy" – the opposite of a bureaucracy – was a 1D model seen as a solution for companies of the future because it embodied a problem-solving mindset.[1] The concept was needed because the bureaucratic approach wasn't – and still isn't – working. Toffler's theory advocated for a system that gave employees greater freedom so they would participate in generating or embracing new ideas. And yet, it was still an approach that only slightly modified traditional organizational structures by putting specialists into market-based project teams, or task forces, to do their work. It was a good idea that didn't go far enough. What kept adhocracy from working was the word's origin – the suffix "cracy" comes from the Greek verb "to govern." Adhocracy has outdated command-and-control overtones.

Employee freedom and creativity are critical aspects of the successful company of the future, but they must be developed within the company's culture rather than mandated. If the philosophy is going to work today, it has to be customer-centered. Cross-functional teams are important, but they need to spring up organically, not artificially. That's what customer-centering will do for an organization's culture. Cultures that are set up to do the right thing require less governing.

Graham Milner, WD-40 senior vice president, says that the

organization realizes that improvements for customers start with the company having a clear set of values that drive the organization. WD-40 uses a hierarchical system of vision, values and knowing who you serve. This system consists of:

- Knowing the value of doing the right thing
- Creating positive lasting memories for customers, building a brand perception on how the WD-40 product has impacted their lives.
- Making it better than it is today

"Making sense" begins with the recognition that meaningful work involves finding a better solution for the customer. The organization of the future will be more solid, built around a foundation that is centered on what makes sense for customers. If the old structure was static, the new version thrives on uncertainty. It is metamorphic: The company is ready to become something else if that's what it takes to connect with customers.

The One Constant

When examining the future of its business, Amazon.com's leaders not only anticipate what will change; they also ask, "What is not going to change in the next five years?" For that company, the one constant is its need to satisfy and delight customers with high value and differentiated products. That is where creative thinking comes into play. Amazon CEO, Jeff Bezos noted, "If in the old world you devoted 30 percent of your attention to building a great service and 70 percent of your attention to shouting about it, in the new world, that inverts. It's important to have some kind of mechanism to figure out if you're wrong about a deeply held precept."[2] Customer-centered thinking is that mechanism.

Customer 3D methods create a climate of self-reliance in every organization. In 3D companies, thinking like a customer is no longer viewed as a distraction from a product focus. On the contrary, it is recognized as an intuitive skill that can be developed, and one that's essential to business success.

It changes the way organizations function by transforming the impersonal style into one that is personal by focusing on common goals with customers. Both the left and the right sides of the brain have their strengths. When integrated, they help businesses reach their full productivity potential while satisfying stakeholders. Blending both through 3D thinking is an investment in organizational energy that will pay high dividends for the future.

In today's business environment, keeping pace requires creative ideas. Product-centered companies struggle with customer changes. The Customer 3D system, on the other hand, introduces an approach that helps the organization see what the future will look like.

Most companies know that to distinguish their products and service from their competitors', they must design and sustain something that is truly different from anything else in the market segment. The trick, of course, is to make certain that this difference is recognized by customers. Your differences must be notable.

The more notable you are, the less susceptible your customers are to the lure of a lower price elsewhere. It's customer performance that's palpable. Amazing outcomes are grounded in a culture of abundance that embodies a willingness to look for ways to add value to customers. It's the kind of treatment that makes customers want to tell 20 of their friends personally or post a story on the web to thousands. Give your customers your best. Be notable.

Reward Loyalty
This applies to customer service, too. People will connect with a company through amazing customer experiences because they have received "something that moves them." 3D companies are beginning to inject fun, imagination and experimentation into their cultures. This creates processes that are memorable and create an emotional connection with customers. Amazon.com, for example, designed a universal "wish list" that lets site users list products they'd like to purchase or receive, whether those products are available on Amazon.com or other sites. Think of it as a not-so-subtle hint to anyone who might buy them a gift. Although Amazon gets no commission from a gift list sale made on another company's site, it realizes that even though buyers leave the Amazon site to make that purchase, they'll come back.

Hyatt Hotels' recognition of its most frequent guests offers another example of 3D performance proactivity. The chain now recognizes

21

its Gold Passport loyalty club members with what it calls "authentic hospitality." Employees are empowered to perform random acts of generosity, including offering complimentary massages or picking up a bar tab for a loyal guest. This is a wise move in light of the fact that elite customers are now expecting higher-end recognition of their status.

To make these rewards more substantial and increase the commitment of already loyal customers, consider leveraging the human side of the relationship. Make them feel even more special through extra services with high-touch, personalized value. Address them from a place of confidence rather with anxiety about whether they will take advantage of you.

These top customers have already proven that they appreciate the value your company offers, so help them build a stronger relationship with you. The new differentiator in growing your bottom line will be your ability to understand the individual preferences of your most loyal customers. The successful companies will give their most loyal customers a reason – and a desire – to tell others how "this company's employees really know me." It's no longer about gathering better information; the secret is in better use of the information that you already have about these premier customers.

Customer Excellence as a Way of Life

Successful companies strive for excellence but their success doesn't come from products and marketing. The secret is in creating this excellence from the viewpoint of the customer, who is the ultimate judge of whether the company delivers on its promise – or not. This comes from being customer-centered.

> We are what we repeatedly do. Excellence, then, is not an act, but a habit.
> *Aristotle*

Pixar Animation Studios is a great example. Its core value is that people in the organization will produce nothing short of excellence in their animation. This approach is liberating because it creates a foundation that gives employees the confidence to make decisions and take creative risks. They are not afraid to challenge the status quo if it will produce a better result for customers. Pixar makes the deliverable the best it can be before the customer experiences it.

One of the cornerstones of Pixar's excellence is its attention to detail. The company uses an unusual amount of research to ensure accuracy and reality. For the animated movie, "Finding Nemo," its commitment to realism drove employees to dissect fish and study their anatomies. Guest lecturers taught them about algae and kelp, jellyfish movement, and underwater translucence.

Pixar gives real authority to the collaborative product development teams. They review each others' work while it's still in progress, inspiring further creativity and ensuring that there are no surprises when the finished product is delivered. In addition, the company has developed an ability to recognize how its customers will use and benefit from the stories it creates. The philosophy is not to invent another platform to sell more toys and fast food meals, but to create the best story and the highest quality animation possible. Sales will follow naturally.

If animated movie fans were told that Pixar was releasing a new film with no mention of the subject, concept, or characters, most would probably say they would be looking forward to seeing it. That is the strength of Pixar's brand reputation. What can we learn from an organization that has one of the highest possible trust levels and favorable brand identities among its customers? Pixar teaches us that excellence is not an act; it's a habit that is ingrained throughout the organization. Excellence is grounded in the premise that the entire organization will think like its customers.

Customer-centered organizations care only about the best outcomes for their customers. 1D companies focusing on profits, on the other hand, never really achieve this high level of admiration from their customers. Customer-centricity begins with a goal of excellence, but it is not based on how good you think you are. Instead, it begins and ends with the willingness to let your customers define how excellent you are and to perform at the highest level in everything the customer experiences.

Re-orienting toward excellence in the eyes of the customer can't be done half-way, with one foot remaining in the product-centric world. The goal is to slowly evolve into an operation that is fully Customer 3D. These organizations don't know what's around the corner as they progress on their journey, but they are confident that when they do turn the corner, they will be ready for whatever they encounter. They know they have the ability and commitment to find solutions their customers need.

3D

Magic Eye. When you glance at a Magic Eye drawing, it appears to be a fuzzy abstract pattern. When focusing behind the image, however, your eyes can perceive a depth to the picture. This allows some points of the pattern to seem nearer to you than others. When this happens, 3D images appear. Your organization has a similar 3D dimension. It's the culture that develops to deliver higher value for the customer. It appears when activities are centered on the customer, rather than the product.

Pattern Detail

Hidden Image

Take a creative new look at your organization. Remove the product that your company sells from the equation (temporarily, of course) and concentrate on the image behind it – what is left, in other words, when the product disappears. Now, create a customer-centered strategy that defines the way that you want customers to see you. Make this strategy detailed and list activities that employees should be doing for customers. But also set your standards higher than today's expectations. Set a goal that stretches the organization and empowers employees. It will help the entire organization understand how it can become more customer-centric after the product is put back into the equation.

Figure 1.3 Image can be found at www.magiceye.com

The Paradox of Letting Go of the Status Quo

Customer 3D organizations are successful because they aren't obsessed with the status quo. They have allowed themselves to move

24

beyond being product-centric. The paradox of the organizations featured in this book is that they already sell products and provide services that are the leaders in their industries. Ironically, they have moved on from what could have turned into a fixation with their products to a new dimension of performance that will make them even stronger in the future.

And yet, 3D is still about pleasing the customer. But because employees have the added dimension available to them – the powerful capability to add value at the organizational level, not just the transactional stage – it makes the ability to please the customer at the "event" level so easy. In other words, they are fully prepared for 1D transactions because they have 3D capabilities "in reserve" and backed by the entire organization.

"Barlean's completely supports me in both educating and pleasing the customer at the same time," says Barb Bloch, customer service representative. "I am empowered to solve customer problems using a 'this is how I would have done it' approach."

3D is cultural and cumulative. It goes beyond product-centering to design and deliver a customer experience that is universal throughout the organization. 1D is almost ubiquitous in today's world. If most organizations are 1D, however, think of the opportunities waiting for you when you become 3D.

TWO

Organically Grown: How Organizations Become Coherent

*Organic growth is more valuable because
it comes from your core competencies.
It's like muscle. If you use it, it gets stronger.*
*A.G. Lafley, former Chairman & CEO,
Procter & Gamble*

There is no detailed owner's manual for organizations that want
to be customer-centered. Instead, the customer-centered state is an
outcome that develops out of strong leadership and a positive culture
offering employees freedom to act on behalf of customers. The
Customer 3D system leads organizations down a path toward a better
understanding of their customers and their needs.

3D companies don't see customers as opponents – instead, this
approach expands the organization's culture to the point where
employees see customers as allies who contribute to their success.
These successes, in turn, help them buy into a stronger future. The
result is an organization that is far more effective than its flat, one-
dimensional counterparts.

Customer-centricity requires that an organization be centered.
Customer 3D is disciplined, but natural at the same time. It creates
super-organisms that are pumped with adrenalin to work for
customer success. These 3D businesses are wide awake and know
what superior performance looks like – and that the picture includes
both leaders and employees that are fully present and engaged.

27

Heliotropism and Customers

When a plant sits in a window, over time, it begins to lean toward the light. This reflects heliotropism – an organism's natural tendency to lean toward the light – positive energy – and away from the dark – negative energy. Eventually, one side of the stem grows rapidly so that it can shift the direction of the flower to face the sun – a phenomenon you'll see in a field of sunflowers as the flower heads follow the sun across the sky throughout the day.

There are a number of organizational studies that prove that generous, abundant behavior creates what experts call an "upward spiral of improvement" similar to what happens with plants and heliotropism. The resulting actions attract customers who observe a corporate behavior designed to improve their lives, not the corporation's internal costs. It creates a sense of attachment that strengthens customer loyalty. Leaders in extraordinary companies believe in always giving more than people expect to receive. In fact, that's the secret: to give unselfishly. If you do it well, you will get your reward sometime later – along with that positive "upward spiral of improvement."

It requires understanding that eliminating customer problems isn't enough because correcting problems is ordinary behavior. Problems can't be ignored, of course. But customers expect organizations to take care of them – that's standard operating procedure. Extraordinary performance comes from enabling customers to succeed; this in turn comes from visualizing service to those customers that never stands still. Educate your culture to believe that your business will attract more and more loyal customers by doing and being what they want and need.

Don't see your company as "just a supplier" to your customers. Be that light in the window – a positive energy source. When you think proactively like your customers, you create an energy source that attracts the right customers in the same way the sun attracts plants. Instead of simply being a one-dimensional provider of goods or services, be the center of an ecosystem that delivers what customers need to be successful.

Customers are attracted to organizations that embody this idea-developing energy. They see them as higher performers. They are legendary, rather than ordinary.

Lessons from Frank Lloyd Wright

Architect Frank Lloyd Wright's success provides an interesting parallel to how organizations can achieve customer-centric success. Wright believed in using open spaces with wide views of the outside. He used casement windows which open fully to the outside, for example, rather than traditional windows which leave half of their space closed even when opened. Everything flows to the outside. His designs always allowed for an abundance of natural light inside. Wright's work embodied the spirit of openness that successful customer connections require.

He also believed that buildings (like customer-centric companies) should fit into their environments, rather than the other way around. Wright wrote, "No house should ever be *on* a hill or *on* anything. It should be *of* the hill. Belonging to it. Hill and house should live together each the happier for the other."[1] This space sharing represents a union for a single purpose – just as the purpose of an organization should complement its customers' needs.

Wright was trying to develop a new, more human center for viewing the world, but it serves as a great customer philosophy, as well. He described its essence this way: "A great architect is not made by way of a brain nearly so much as he is made by way of a cultivated, enriched heart."[2] By 1908, he was using the word "organic" to describe his approach to integrating space and function into a coherent whole.

Frank Lloyd Wright worked a lifetime to develop the architectural character of his buildings that were designed to achieve flexibility and abundance. His passion for a harmonious relationship between design and function provides a great lesson for customer-centricity. Just as he saw everything that he designed as one with its environment, customer-centered organizations exist to enhance the overall success of their customers.

Better than a Machine

A vibrant, customer-centered organization's qualities are represented

29

by words and phrases that employees of organizations featured in this book use to describe their companies. They include:

- Responsive
- Empowering
- Strength of purpose
- Giving
- Natural
- Innovative
- Resourceful

These aren't words people use to describe 1D organizations, which often have a more mechanistic or impersonal view. In contrast, 3D companies have chosen to expand to a new, more humanistic dimension. They ignore the traditional rules if those rules get in the way of serving customers properly. Like architect Wright, they have taken a new view of the world, one that sees things in their wholeness, not as fragments or parts of a machine.

> Mechanization best serves mediocrity.
> *Frank Lloyd Wright*

This view starts with the leaders. Most 3D leaders believe they belong to an organization with some degree of life. 3D leaders want to be the architect that creates a system that will sustain itself when it's fully connected with customers. This type of leader believes in and models these qualities as core values. As Garry Ridge of WD-40 says, "One of my passions about leaders is that they don't 'sit and quit.' Leaders must educate if they want the tribe to be enduring." Many of us have experienced organizations like this that are more alive than others. We haven't had a name for those qualities until now – it's Customer 3D.

It's about delivering life, rather than products and procedures. It feels healthier. It makes us feel more comfortable because we recognize that these companies are honest, genuine, and authentic. As customers, we feel the wholeness and respond to it. We hear a voice speaking from the heart. Our spirits are enlarged when we do business with companies like this because we connect with an identifiable structure in the culture of the business. It may be contrary to what we have been taught, but we connect with it and commit to it more deeply.

The Power of Vision

In 3D companies, organizational structure isn't important. What really matters is the ability to align facilities, departments and teams to properly serve customers.

At Barlean's Organic Oils, the first person with customer contact "owns" that particular customer. While Barlean's has a traditional departmental structure, it overcomes silo behavior with a culture that encourages doing what makes sense for customers. Everyone has an equal part.

Organizations will not be successful by making old ways more efficient. The competitive environment is changing so rapidly that a lean cost structure is no longer a differentiator. Instead, the advantage going forward will go to the companies that can develop a solidly different vision that tests their decisions based on what is best for customers. 3D organizations have a clear understanding of what part their customers play in their company's vision.

Leadership must establish what the future will look like, and then determine how today's and tomorrow's actions will help them achieve this future. 3D leaders understand how customers will be involved when they position the business for the future. After that, they establish metrics and milestones that will indicate how successful they are at continually improving customer connections.

The Customer 3D system helps an organization sort through all of the alternatives – including fads – to concentrate on only those that will support a customer-centered future. Rather than paying lip service to customer service, a company with a vision that's committed to its customers bases all of its decisions on how they will impact customers. Unfortunately, even when their vision statements mention customers, too many 1D companies go after this vision through low level acts of customer service that represent good transactional performance, but aren't game-changing.

In *Hope Is Not a Method*,[3] the authors refer to this technique as "making yesterday perfect." They describe the General Electric of 1981, when Jack Welch took over, as one that had "perfected the management model of the 1950s." In other words, prior to Welch,

31

GE wasn't a forward-looking company.

Rather than reengineering old products and processes as the pre-Welch GE did, 21st Century organizations must change the way they change. Working harder to do the same things better will not lead to success. Leaders can't build winning organizations by simply adapting to accommodate what's around them. They need to follow the example of 3D companies that are building winning organizations by re-orienting to develop closer customer connections. Clearly, the 3D approach to bringing about enduring change by focusing organizations on solutions that are important to their customers is the winning option.

> **If we don't change direction soon, we'll end up where we're going.**
> *Irwin Corey*

The future is created by positive steps, not wishful thinking. The danger of not taking strong actions is not in losing your customers, although that will happen in the long run if you cling to old mindsets. The danger is in failing them when failing equates to not continually improving based on what customers need and value to make their lives better. Organizations that integrate this thinking into their cultures create employee change agents who know how to think like a customer at every touch point.

3D leaders focus their organizations on customer success. They manage and reinforce this purpose by making certain that every internal process is performed correctly and efficiently. They know that they must create the future and articulate a vision by demonstrating a line of sight between today's marginal improvements and the desired future quantum improvements for customers. This future destination creates a context within which the organization can act.

This vision inspires commitment in employees to something larger than themselves. It gives them a strong sense of purpose. They are building cathedrals instead of merely cutting stones, as the old saying goes. Vision is a challenging concept because it forces people to change. When the efforts are directed toward the customer, though, that kind of change becomes transformational.

32

To be successful, a vision also must be empowering. But that becomes second nature when employees embrace actions designed to create a future that will delight their customers. The Customer 3D system provides the basis to use when looking ahead to the future instead

> The purpose of an organization is to enable common men to do uncommon things.
> *Peter Drucker*

of guarding the status quo. Be a builder, not a maintainer. Don't rethink your vision; instead, re-orient the commitment behind that vision through your customers.

The Impossibility Question Process

You have a vision to transform your organization into the most customer-centered player in your industry. The problem is convincing everyone else in your company that it's possible. Sound familiar? Here's one approach that will help. It's a successful, thought-provoking exercise that we use in our client sessions.

The Impossibility Question (IQ)[4] is a technique used to focus on solutions to problems that, at first, seem like insurmountable challenges. It helps a person or group who are wavering between fear ("this is a threatening idea that will fail and ruin me") and apathy ("this might be a good idea, but it sounds like too much effort on my part") to look at change differently. The catalyst can be developed with two simple questions:

> **Question 1:** "What is something that is impossible (or that we will never achieve)?"
>
> Let's assume for this exercise that the answer is: "Our company will never become truly customer-centered."
>
> To get the person from a place where he's offering excuses to one where he's having a positive attitude about a possible future state, you must make him picture that future as a reality. It's time to ask the second question.
>
> **Question 2:** "What would make it possible?"
>
> This will get them to shift to moving in a positive direction. Possible responses include:

33

- "We could interview customers, observe how they are using our product or service, and design new features that would make the product easier to use."
- "We could meet every morning to discuss how we make our processes easier for customers to understand and use."
- "We could involve customers in our new employee hiring process."

Questioning works better than telling when there's a challenge to overcome. It creates buy-in when the team you're working with figures out how to approach the goal more realistically – even if it's only by taking the initial steps in the right direction. It will help them picture what the destination looks like and enable them to buy into the idea that getting there is possible.

The exercise also asks the team to articulate how the ideas they offer will result in a stronger relationship with customers, and how that benefits everyone. The shift in perspective starts to take on a life of its own as people see – and believe – that they can do it.

The Impossibility Question process will start your company toward doing something about solving problems that were thought to be unsolvable. Instilling customer-centricity into your organization's culture is not impossible, of course, but for those who struggle to see solutions, this method offers a powerful tool for overcoming negativity. It can jumpstart your organization's efforts to think like a customer and dramatically increase your success.

Creating Employee Attitudes

After using the Impossibility Question process to overcome obstacles and negativity, your business is closer to becoming one that is Customer 3D. 3D organizations are great places to work because their leaders have defined customer-centricity as "everybody is your customer," whether "everybody" is inside or outside the company. This belief creates a deeply personal attitude among employees.

cSubs has an employee motivation program that goes a long way toward shaping employee attitudes. The program, which allows the subscription management company to thank employees for customer-centered performance, includes a vacation incentive awards program that distributes " cSubs points" at a quarterly pizza party. Points are rewarded for employee achievements that are shared at these events; these accomplishments might include getting compliments from clients, helping the company find and hire a new employee, recruiting new clients, going above and beyond, identifying ways to increase efficiencies at work, helping to reduce costs, or performing community service work. When they accumulate enough points, employees can exchange them for vacation trips.

Proud of the program, President Julie Auslander says, "Acknowledging, rewarding and celebrating our success in this way has been key to our growth." Employees, she says, appreciate that their efforts are recognized and rewarded and this, in turn, reinforces their commitment to making a difference for customers.

Context Provides a Big Advantage

3D companies also need customer context. The phrase "taken out of context" has negative overtones, suggesting situations when we're misquoted or when inaccurate information is shared and causes problems. If "taken out of context" is bad for business, where does "putting it in context" fit? It's good. And the context that you need comes from thinking like a customer.

Here's the reason that you want context from your customers: There is no greater source of new opportunities. Forget what you thought you knew about being customer-focused. The new business model is built around a culture in which employees are customer-centered in a way that helps them see innovations that will benefit the customer. The goal is to constantly search for ways to use decisions people make every day to improve customer closeness. You get the information you need from knowing your customers.

Executives in 1D businesses have gotten used to operating from "maps" that are too narrowly focused. In *Wired to Care*[5], Dev Patnaik observes that over-simplified data and lack of context lead to a disconnection from customers. He uses the example of Harry Beck's map of the London Underground. The map is brilliant in its visual illustration of the subway lines, but fails to point out important details, including the fact that people can walk between certain stations faster than they can take the train. The "maps" that

35

businesses use are abstract; companies can take actions that seem sensible based on those maps, but the maps simply aren't suited to the real world.

Similarly, shortcuts and overly simplified information cause organizations to begin to lose touch with reality, which can lead to bad decisions. They won't head in the proper direction without incorporating the most important factor that is left off the maps – customers. Customer 3D shows organizations how to walk in the shoes of their customers.

Patnaik's book describes a classroom exercise he calls "Needfinding." It uses role playing to demonstrate first how to find customer needs and then design ways to meet them. It relies on context to give meaning to the solution and to help identify potential improvements. According to Patnaik, research shows that students who solve problems in isolation from their partners frequently come up with unique ideas, but these ideas often don't meet the partners' needs. On the other hand, those who fully understand their partners often find a way to meet a need that the partners didn't know they had. This exercise hints at a concept that is essential to success for every company today: value creation. It requires knowing as much about customers as possible.

We are surrounded by plenty of information, but, without customer context, the danger is that decisions will be made only from the viewpoint of how they will benefit the company. Customer context provides a valuable reference point. It validates a company's decisions about what is most valuable and practical for its customers.

One of the most straightforward examples is the mail-order video rental service Netflix. Because it provides employees with a free subscription, they experience what their customers go through when ordering and returning DVDs. This firsthand experience with the process provides the context that allows them to generate a number of process improvements and ideas for new services that will benefit all customers.

Consider the challenge Dr. Martin Luther King, Jr. gave us: "Life's most urgent question is: What are you doing for others?" Organizations that adopt this attitude will learn to listen to their

36

customers and feel what they're feeling. The essence of being customer-centered is knowing the full context in which your customers live and operate. By evaluating opportunities in the context of customers, your organization will increase its potential for generating new ideas. This will lead to a huge advantage that could include new growth platforms and real differentiation from your competition.

Deeply-Rooted Culture

Many companies believe that they can develop a customer-focused organization through a command-and-control approach. The reality is that an organization will never become customer-centered without a deep-rooted culture that allows it to flourish.

3D companies have a solid foundation. In *The Roots of Aliveness*[6], Michael Jones uses the ecology of a tree as a metaphor for business success. Here's how he describes the process that most business strategies operate under: "The outer life (of the tree) is symbolized by the leaves and branches; they correspond to a life of reactivity and busy-ness – of action plans, performance goals, desired outcomes and results." This reactive focus is the approach that consumes 1D organizations. Sometimes these companies direct their attention down a little, to the trunk and lower limbs. Here they look at structures, strategies and processes. Jones continues, "Where we spend the least of our time is the ground underneath. Yet it is the roots and the soil that give the tree resilience and the strength to grow and weather *sudden* changes year after year."

The 3D corporate culture is like a tree's root system. Instead of getting caught up in the false feeling that machine-like control, with no adaptation, leads to success, the culture learns, like roots, to sense and absorb. Root systems know how to, as Jones[7] explains it, "invent and change course" as needed to benefit the entire plant. Like those roots, being customer-centered requires being open to what is emerging and more alive and a willingness to accept more possibilities. Being customer-centered is not mechanistic; it is natural.

Just as a plant's growth is dependent on its root structure, companies must be deeply rooted within values and purpose that enrich their

37

growth before they can blend with their environments and customers. With customer-centered leaders who help establish the organization's values and their execution, and employees who have the freedom to support those values, the organization has the right foundation to grow stronger.

Is Your Culture Authentic?

It can be difficult to understand how we are seen by our customers. It can be equally dangerous to think that our mission/vision statements automatically translate into the image our customers have of us. Truthfully, our customers' perceptions are much closer to what we really are, not what we choose to believe we are.

Figure 2.1 originally appeared in Henri Matisse's 1947 essay, "Exactitude is not Truth.[8]" Although these self-portraits are clearly different from each other, we can readily observe that they are all the same man. They share a common quality that is recognizable. Matisse describes it this way: "Everything has an inherent truth, which must be distinguished from its surface appearance." The different elements in the four drawings "translate . . . the organic makeup of the person depicted."

Figure 2.1

Similarly, every organization emits subtle – and not so subtle – information about what it represents and how it will behave or react in any given situation. Call it the company's "essence" or "sensibility" or something else. Every organization gives off information about what's at its core; this is picked up by customers. In 1D, product-centric cultures, that core quality is often a sales mentality that suggests there's just one "Matisse" – one image for the entire company. 3D, customer-centered cultures recognize that while they have a single identity, it manifests itself with diverse, thinking-like-a-customer performances.

This essence is what customer-centric businesses develop and deliver to differentiate themselves from product-centered competitors. Businesses might pretend to be one thing or attempt to brand themselves with impressive taglines, but customers will see through these facades if they are not authentic. If the sensibility of an organization is "all about the product," then overtures to the customer will seem shallow and perhaps not genuine. Companies that create a culture that thinks about the customer first will emit a spirit that will instill a new level of life and energy – one that customers find compelling.

Just as there is in the Matisse self portrait, there is a wholeness in every organization. This wholeness is produced from individual elements – people, policies, procedures – that

> Individuality is only possible if it unfolds from wholeness.
> *David Bohm*

can vary tremendously. But there is a character, an essence, which runs deeper than specific features. There is a pattern in the four pictures of Matisse that allows us to recognize him. Likewise, in organizations, there is a wholeness that customers recognize no matter who is delivering the product or service. This wholeness determines everything about the organization, including the customer experience. When that wholeness is built around a product, it is one-dimensional. When the purpose of the organization is built around the customer, with the product becoming secondary, then it becomes three-dimensional. Matisse calls this the "essential truth," the only truth that matters.

Resourceful Leadership

This "essence" that many customer-centric organizations share is a resourceful culture. It starts with the organization's leaders. Their vision is practical, and even frugal, and it translates into the culture of everyone working there. The message is clear: "Focus on our customers rather than ourselves."

Bruce Barlean, one of the owners of Barlean's Organic Oils, has created an organization that is sensible, rather than fancy, and loved

39

by its customers. Its leadership operates with a generous, abundant philosophy focused on "just do the right thing and the results will follow." Employees are super-responsive and passionate about working with customers to educate them and help them live healthier lives.

Conversely, in the face of this abundant philosophy toward customers and employees, Barlean's is frugal with its internal spending. When water tanks were needed to create an emergency watering system at the manufacturing plant, employees built an ingenious system themselves with a relatively small investment. It was far more cost effective than purchasing expensive water towers. When the marketing department wanted to put neck hangers on every bottle, one of the leaders designed and built a machine to do it that cost less than buying one.

All customer-centered businesses have confidence in their capabilities and inventiveness. Their leaders educate the organization by modeling creativity and calling on inner resources to take care of nearly every situation. Resourcefulness sends a three-part message to employees:

1. We, as an organization, are bright, talented, creative and capable of handling all situations.
2. We want to spend our money on our customers and employees. We will have to spend on equipment and supplies, of course, but we are capable of using our ingenuity to keep those costs to a minimum.
3. Never take circumstances at face value. Use your imagination and creativity to solve problems and be open to new ideas.

Can frugality and generosity co-exist? In product-centered companies, frugality manifests itself as cost-cutting and generosity as "giving away the store." But in customer-centered companies, these two concepts actually complement each other. They become core values that represent sensibility and that reinforce the purpose of a stronger, better life for customers and employees, while still addressing the bottom line. They aren't restrictive concepts – they are expansive and synonymous with the imagination that makes customer-focused businesses more successful than their counterparts.

Find Your Fire

Nobody wants to skimp on customer relationships. Because they are ever-changing, though, understanding certain universal and timeless principles will help us avoid being pulled in directions that are too short-term.

Legendary architect Christopher Alexander believed that when we began creating structures and communities that no longer touched the humanitarian elements of our nature, we lost our "fire." In response, Alexander developed an approach that made sense of the repetition and variety in our cities and towns. This "language" of proper space and geometry, he says, "gives people who use it the power to create an infinite variety of new and unique buildings."[9] His synthesis, referred to as "the architecture of humanism," shepherded in techniques that offered a feeling of amplitude or fullness.

There is an essential property to any system that accounts for its wholeness. In architecture, it's your awareness of how a building's space is used in just the right way. It's a satisfying, abundant feeling that delights us as the building's customers when we experience it. There's something similar, too, in customer relationship systems.

In parallel with Alexander's work, many organizations have lost a fundamental quality of great customer relations – congruence with customers. It's satisfying to customers – not in that they fundamentally like the product or service that you provide, but that they feel deeply satisfied with their decision to do business with you. It's the difference between the feeling you get when you do just enough to satisfy customers and what you experience when you completely connect with them. It's the feeling of freedom that arrives when you know that your customers have discovered they have absolutely made the right decision. Creating the right customer relationship system involves building into businesses Alexander's "infinite power" to design unique products and services. When implemented properly, it will take your business to the next level.

Employees love working for 3D organizations that have found their "fire." Barb Bloch, customer service representative of Barlean's, notes, "It can be a very stressful when you work for a company that only wants to make money, rather than for an organization that wants to help people. Bruce (the owner) is into helping people."

41

This focused leadership allows the organization to be very giving to employees and customers. "Customers call us just to talk with us because they like us and trust us. There is no timeline about how long we can talk with them; we are allowed to have as long of a conversation as they want," adds Bloch. "We can take the time to do the job right."

The future will belong to those organizations that can grasp these universal concepts and find their fire. Our role should be to constantly move our organizations closer to a system that is more natural and whole. First, you understand it. Then you figure out how to pursue it. It will dramatically change the way you relate to customers.

3D

View-Master. The world met the View-Master at the New York World's Fair in 1939. Although now considered a children's toy, it was originally intended as an alternative to the scenic postcard and primarily used disks with views of tourist attractions such as the Grand Canyon. Now owned by Mattel Toys subsidiary Fisher-Price, it was one of the original inductees in the National Toy Hall of Fame at The Strong. It has long provided a new way of viewing in which the mind could see a third dimension, beyond the flatness of a traditional picture.

Take a "snapshot" of a process you deliver to your customers in a very traditional way. How could adding fun to that process increase the word-of-mouth marketing by customers who will be so thrilled that they tell others about the unique experience you have provided?

Figure 2.2

Image courtesy of Fisher-Price

What's Wrong with Being Product-Centered?

The number of customer-centered cultures will increase when organizations realize that customers are disappearing because organizations are product-centered.

1D companies look at customer interactions in terms of what they can accomplish by selling their products. They either do what their customers ask them, when the request falls under their procedures, or choose not to do what the customer asks when it doesn't fit under their parameters. 3D organizations, on the other hand, measure their success by what they have helped their customers accomplish.

One dimensional businesses think in terms of functional separation, because they believe that structure allows them to operate efficiently. Thus, the tendency for silos to develop happens quite a lot.

Internally, one-dimensional companies are organized by the services each department delivers, so the customer must navigate through its system to ask a question or get a problem solved. A more treacherous approach might even discourage the call in the first place. It's the ultimate irony when organizations believe that discouraging calls from customers actually improves efficiencies and lowers costs.

But this product-centric approach is out-of-date. The product-centric mentality (even if the "product" is a service) is focused on the provider. It puts the provider above the customer, not in harmony with them on the same level.

What would be a more positive approach? What if, on a call to an organization, you could connect with an individual who had access to a shared system that could personalize the answers to your inquiry based on the organization's knowledge of you and a shared resource of information based on other requests similar to yours? Would you like that system better? This is thinking like a customer. The product-centric mentality (even if the "product" is a service) is focused on the provider. It puts the provider above the customer, not in harmony with them on the same level.

The customer-centric system is focused on making life easier for the consumer. The irony, of course, is that being customer-centric can be more efficient for the provider than being product-centric. If, as a consumer or customer, you encounter a different person with every transaction, you have to start from the beginning every time. Now, contrast that a situation where you're always served by the same

43

person. You have a relationship with him or her. Your transaction is then based on what he already knows about your preferences. Applying that concept to a bank teller who serves the same customer 52 weeks per year, don't you think the bank's performance is going to be more consistent and more efficient than if you were served by a different teller each time?

Becoming customer-centric is transformational. It improves the supplier's performance as much as it improves customer satisfaction. That's why organizations move in this direction. Using techniques that help the organization think like a customer not only changes the culture, they also make that organization more efficient and effective. What companies have you seen transform themselves into successful, customer-centric powerhouses?

Fluency

Sometimes, the problem with product-centered cultures is that it can feel as if the supplier and the customer don't speak the same language. Think of customer-centricity as a new language you want to learn. You don't want your delivery to be choppy or awkward, or to rely on just a handful of words or phrases. You want to be fluent. Fluency in a language requires superior comprehension and delivery skills. Fluency in customer-centric service requires similar smoothness. In both cases, your fluency is ultimately judged by the other person, not by you.

The Strong, a Rochester, N.Y. organization known for its National Museum of Play, is widely admired for its customer focus. The museum's collections include hundreds of thousands of historical objects related to play, including the world's largest and most comprehensive collection of dolls, toys, and games. Tens of thousands of artifacts are on view in museum exhibits and thousands more are viewable online.

Its "Guest Services" program emphasizes to employees that they must provide a high level of personalized service – and they are empowered to do so. If, for example, an autistic child is intimidated by the constant stimulation in the main museum, a museum host might suggest that the family explore the Toy Hall of Fame for a quieter experience. This empowered culture also encourages

44

hosts to implement new ideas to help customers without asking for supervisor permission first. For example, when an admissions desk manager realized he was abandoning the people waiting in line when he stepped away to make announcements about a regular program location, he found a solution on his own. He pre-recorded the location announcement so he could play it with the touch of a button, and told his supervisor about it later.

The Strong works to continuously improve the customer – or "guest" – experience. This fluency in meeting customer needs has led to tremendous organizational growth as employees accept new challenges in the same way that lifetime language learners look for new ways to become more eloquent with their speech. This growth process included acknowledging that its customers were a diverse group that included not only museum-goers – children, parents, grandparents and nostalgia buffs – but researchers and collectors, too.

Product-centric companies expect customers to be fluent in their language. If you travel someplace where they speak another language and expect them to understand you and respond appropriately, you will be disappointed. Customer fluency is grounded in sharing a common language – the language that your customer knows and understands. And, while you might feel good about your new language skills, the native speaker is the best judge of your proficiency. As your customer-centered fluency improves, your organization will become more motivated to continue the learning process. Being a customer-centric organization is predicated on making progress every day; to become fluent, you must practice.

Success requires collaboration so that your organization is speaking the customer's language. But it goes far beyond learning enough words and phrases to get by. If you're not thinking like a customer, you won't be able to sustain your results. The conversation will break down. Focusing on customers is the most important dimension of your organization's culture, and your customer service delivery must be as fluent as possible.

Customers are Changing

There has been a fundamental shift in how organizations must   45 behave to keep customers and it goes beyond fluency. Cutting-edge strategies take into account that customers in every market are going to keep changing; it's how it is. So why try to relate to them with a static, rules-driven culture? What worked for your customers in the past might not work today. Flexibility is the new goal. As MacKenzie Shirm, cSubs customer support representative, notes, "We have rules, of course, to create structure so things run smoothly. However, we rarely use the words 'policy' and 'procedure' because of the negativity associated with them. Instead, we convey how much we try to do for them. When, for example, a publisher is not willing to be flexible, we immediately think about what we can do and begin to explore other options."

It's important to challenge traditional business measurement methods and their ability to keep pace with change. In general, they don't usually produce behaviors that connect employees to their work or generate a shared sense of what's best for customers. Visionary leaders understand that even though established measures are no longer working, feedback is still important to the vitality and adaptability of an organization – in the same way that it is to any living system. In Chapter 7, we explain a new approach to measurement, the Customer 3D Index. It's a flexible way to measure a customer-centered organization's pro-activity level and develop ways to improve it.

Leaders need to gather and apply information that will help their organizations adapt and thrive. They can't assume that the success of the past will continue in the future. A "context dependent" culture learns new questions to ask so the business can hone its performance. It fosters an environment in which customers and organizations can co-evolve and stay connected.

What has value to your customers? This is feedback that's incredibly important. Value relates to how the customer feels about doing business with you. It's your "fit" with the customer's needs; it's embodied in an emotional connection. Execution involves a deep understanding of those needs and a high degree of flexibility because fit is judged by your delivery in its broadest, most proactive, sense. What if you could promise your customers that you will always look for better value for them – and mean it, even when their wants and

46

needs continually change? If you aren't articulating this customer flexibility philosophy to your organization, you are voting with silence for business-as-usual. Are you sure you want the message to be that you're really product-centric?

The challenge for the future is to stay ahead of changing customer expectations. The solution is a customer-centered system that's flexible enough to allow you to continually re-evaluate how you deal with customers. With this approach, your organization can learn how to focus on adaptability and growth, rather than stability and control. If your customers are changing, you need a customer-centered system that allows you to anticipate their needs and change with them if you want to achieve superior performance. The most powerful message you can send customers is that you are capable of changing with them.

Are Your Ideas Obsolete?

It's been said that there will be more changes in the next 30 years than there has been in the previous 300. Not many of us find that surprising. Still, it's difficult for most organizations to see how these changes and intersecting trends apply to them and their customer relationships. Frankly, it's perplexing to imagine scenarios in which the ideas that made your company successful become extinct.

The danger, of course, from a supplier's standpoint is that not responding to these changes can cause you to set expectations for customer needs too low. It's easy to think that customers only want what we have been giving them all along. This is "status quo bias" – people prefer to leave things the way they are. 3D organizations counter this with a passion for originality.

For example, MacKenzie Shirm of cSubs says, "We want to do something unique for them that they've never seen before." She describes a client's employee portal that includes access to cSubs services. "They were trying to place a large order for books, which was subject to approval limits. We saved them a lot of work by making a programming change on this portal so this process could work. Now, the system is there for the future for any bulk orders – and it's transferable to other clients," she says.

Certainly, your organization's daily operation includes ideas that

47

are trending toward obsolete. But they're hard to spot and frankly, it's difficult to admit that our one-dimensional assumptions about customers that are ingrained in our organizations – those concepts that people never question – might not be valid anymore. The more we clear out the cobwebs in our minds, the less disruptive the years ahead will be. Because we are faced with so many more complexities and alternative trends than in the past, overcoming the blind spots requires a solution that's fact-based.

Make sure that your organization is prepared for change by putting customer-centered monitors in place that will condition everyone to look for new ways by questioning the old ones. Install your own GPS system to recognize when a better route is available. Set up a process to pull information from the marketplace and to evaluate change on customers' terms, not yours. This process is not about gloom and doom. Just the opposite – it will be a great platform for starting discussions about ways to strengthen your organization by consistently looking for opportunities to outperform.

3D organizations have the confidence to find and replace traditional ideas with dynamic, customer-centered ideas that will shape a new direction. When these ideas are grounded in customer needs, they have a phenomenally greater chance of survival. In essence, the organization's flexibility delivers security for the future. Imagine a delivery model in which your customers never feel as if they have to sacrifice anything because you are keeping them at the leading edge of new ideas. It's powerful, isn't it?

It's difficult to gauge the impact of change while it is happening because you're too close to it. Don't let success lead to arrogance because that will prevent you from asking how long yesterday's ideas will stay viable. Instead, the Customer 3D system will help you become aware of challenges to your current ideas while it allows your organization to adapt to its customers.

Attracting the Right Customers

Can you be customer-centered and still be selective about your customers? You can, but it's not as simple as rejecting certain types of customers. Instead, it involves defining the most desirable behaviors in the community of customers that you serve and

48

guiding your current and future customers to grow in ways that will galvanize the relationship. Customer-centricity goes well beyond 1D reactivity to customer needs. It also involves injecting some fun and proactively transforming your customers by empowering them in their relationship with your organization.

Years ago, management guru Peter Drucker said, "The purpose of a business is to create a customer.[10]" In today's business environment, this concept takes on another level of meaning because companies can actually create the types of customers they connect with best. With this process today, you:

1. Develop a proactive, customer-centered business that's focused on making its customers better.
2. Identify the customers that really connect with this business model and that are most likely to challenge you to perform at a higher level. Think of these customers as connectors who want a true relationship with your company because of shared values.
3. Create and attract more customers just like them by convincing others to enjoy what you are providing.

Connectors can be defined by what they do and how they act – not by who they are or how much they spend. They are the ones who want to engage with your organization. Develop your own customer-centered culture and shared values, show it to customers at every touch point, and connect with those customers who appreciate those values and want to grow the relationship.

Really great customers are the ones who want to develop closer partnerships with their suppliers. Consider the brilliance of Maker's Mark Bourbon's Ambassador Program.

> If it's not fun, why do it?
> *Corporate motto,*
> *Ben & Jerry's Ice Cream*

This initiative that uses special mailings and gifts to encourage fans to introduce friends to the brand goes far beyond an arms-length sales transaction to engage. As a member, my wife has received business cards, wrapping paper, and even a certificate for a barrel of bourbon that was named for her. She feels connected to the brand

because of this program. Success today and in the future depends

49

not on serving just anyone who will buy from you, but attracting more customers like your best customers – and for Maker's Mark, that's people like my wife. They are using her – and others in the Ambassador Program – to find others like her who appreciate their values and might see them as extraordinary.

Here's how to connect with customers in ways that will encourage them to connect others with you, in return: introduce them to the unexpected on a consistent basis. Shower them with new products, services, fun approaches, great information, and creative ideas. Do things that say "thank you." Give customers something that will be highly anticipated. Barlean's, for instance, has an anniversary bottle with the customer's name and a picture of the owners. Fun ideas help honor customers and make them feel special. They will end up not only enjoying the ride, but expecting this type of relationship from other suppliers. When most of those suppliers aren't able to provide this type of experience, they will look bad – and you will look better.

Customer-centricity has a benefit that most organizations don't fully understand or utilize. It is understanding, at a deep level, what your ideal customers do, how they behave, and the personality traits that you want to encourage in them. This knowledge gives you the ability to shape your deliverables so that they develop existing customers and attract new ones who are just like them. These are the customers who transcend their role as buyers to become customers who truly connect with you.

THREE

The Inside Story:
Working for 3D Organizations from
the Employee Perspective

I have been impressed with the urgency of doing.
Knowing is not enough; we must apply.
Being willing is not enough; we must do.
Leonardo da Vinci

When employees believe that their organization allows them to create extraordinary results for their customers, the company is more successful. That is the principle that powers 3D momentum. In contrast, employees of 1D businesses are conditioned to think only about products and procedures. They see customer needs only from the perspective of the product offering. Even if employees are able to take a broader view of what customers want, they appear as actors trying to perform for an audience in a restricted setting, unable to offer the performance they know they are capable of.

3D employees, on the other hand, feel a sense of purpose that is based on the organization's vision. They view their jobs differently because the culture allows them – even empowers them – to care for the customer. They exist to serve the customer. The Customer 3D approach allows an organization to act like a small business in terms of customer relationships – even if it has thousands or hundreds of thousands of employees – because it champions customer-centered behavior.

Doing Meaningful Work
Successful 3D organizations have a culture in which, as business

51

author Jim Collins describes it, "People do not have jobs; they have responsibilities."[1] At lubricant company WD-40, doing meaningful work that makes a difference is one of the company's five core values. With products that include Lava Soap, 3-in-One Oil and the legendary WD-40 lubricant, CEO Garry Ridge tells employees they are in the "squeak, smell, and dirt business." Their goal is eliminating these problems for customers. Rather than simply producing and selling these products, employees understand that they are improving the quality of life for their customers.

We all want to carry out meaningful work. That's what a culture of customer-centricity does for organizations. It empowers employees to express their identity and act individually in such a way that they put their stamp on the organization by building a stronger presence for the customer. They go beyond merely doing their jobs to meeting customer needs in a significant way. Customer-centricity leads to the customer's inclusion in the steps the company takes to improve its business.

What's the litmus test for knowing if your organization is customer-centered? It's how your employees view their jobs. One of Barlean's Organic Oil's customer service representatives describes the company as staffed with passionate, driven people who look for ways to add value to the conversation. He says that his colleagues see themselves as solutions-providers, going beyond what customers expect to provide valuable information. They see themselves as available and responsive.

An employee of one of our healthcare industry clients explained how she can tell the difference between the organization's employees who are people-centered and those who aren't. Given the task of helping a patient to move, the employees who are stuck in a 1D mindset believe they're serving simply by "pushing the wheelchair across the room." The staff members who are really committed to customer-centered 3D performance, on the other hand, see themselves as "helping the patient to get to the other side of the room." The act is the same, but the quality of the customer connection is much greater with the generous 3D attitude.

Many of us have heard the story of the traveler who asks three stone cutters, "What are you doing with these stones?" The first worker responds, "I am a stone cutter and I am cutting stones." The second explains, "I am a stone cutter and I am trying to make enough money to support my family." The third answers, "I am a stone cutter and I am building a cathedral." Obviously, these workers have three very different views of the bigger picture. Our clients in all industries want to have more of those cathedral-builders.

WD-40 senior vice-president Graham Milner gets somewhat philosophical when asked about the company's people doing purposeful work that "makes a difference." He has traveled extensively in Latin America and Asia and has "seen families who are working on our behalf benefit themselves. They are economically changed over time by selling WD-40 and their children are better off." Milner says, "We are the stewards of something that is exceptional. It is impactful in people's everyday life and making it easier for them."

Behave Like a Family
CEO Garry Ridge is clear in his direction for the WD-40 business and creating meaningful work for its employees. "Our goal," he says in *Helping People Win at Work*,[2] "is to succeed as a tribe, while acting like a team. A tribe, to reference Maslow's theory, is centered on love and belonging." Once that is in place, then self-esteem happens. "We are an organization where people feel they belong. People are cared about and have a mutual respect," he notes. "The deliverable is that we have 93 percent employee engagement, whereas the average organization has around 30 percent employee commitment. I can't imagine working at an organization where 70 percent of the employees are not committed to the success and purpose of the company."

Barlean's customer service representative Art Morgan selected "family" when asked to select one word to describe working at the company. "Sometimes we can be brutally honest with each other, but we are all treated like family. We bring pot luck dishes to our monthly meetings so that we can enjoy the get-together as a family would," he says. Colleague Sarah Willett adds, "Employees are treated positively all of the time – not only if they are excelling. They are looked on as just as valuable to the company if they are going

53

through some difficulties. This is a family-first company."

Proximity Is Huge

Part of the family-like feeling in 3D organizations is created by employee interaction. 3D organizations know that to maintain a vibrant family, proximity is huge. With that in mind, they encourage a strong community among workers and a feeling of alignment between individuals and departments.

When Microsoft hired interior designer Martha Clarkson to give the company's interior a much-needed facelift, she started by tackling the easy things like paint and wallpaper. Some groups, though, started asking for specific improvements, which helped her realize that she didn't really know with certainty what her colleagues wanted or needed in their work areas. To fix this, Clarkson and her team created a two-year, worldwide research project to "validate what people were telling us." It led to a design effort called Workplace Advantage (WPA) to create communities within the organization.

Because one size doesn't fit all when workgroups are so different, the WPA approach has been to design a variety of spaces for a variety of work styles. Today, Clarkson's team engages with groups a year in advance of actual changes. The work environment design now helps create a feeling of family, one that reflects the personality of each group occupying each space. A hub-style layout that encourages collaboration has contributed to greater transparency, with a cross-group functionality and permeability that gets all people connected.

Proximity is important to the innovation process. Product groups have a very face-to-face culture. People want to be near each other and, with 10 buildings in Microsoft's headquarters complex, Workplace Advantage helps to cluster groups together in the same area of the campus. Clarkson says, "Our job is to use re-design to help them grow."

Innovation doesn't happen in a vacuum. It thrives on proximity. What is different about Microsoft is its investment in design thinking for workspaces – both in dollars and in belief. The company has gone beyond simply supporting it; it has created a Global Workplace Strategies team that is developing ideas for the future. "In other

54

organizations," she notes, "when there are roles like mine, they are usually tasked. Our activities are given more freedom to make positive change happen for employees."

Behaving Like a Community

3D companies are far from insular. They are connected to their communities. At WD-40, this community is a fan club with more than 150,000 members. So that it can interact with these customers as much as possible, the company is designing software that will create a crowdsourcing environment. Customers will be able to submit new ideas, review those submitted by others, and vote for those they think are the best.

When end-users discover he works for WD-40, they share stories of how they have used the product and how much they value it. With a "USE WD40" license plate, other drivers often give him a friendly wave. Once, when stopped at a traffic light, the truck driver next to Milner showed him the can of WD-40 in his cab. At Barlean's, what isn't used in the manufacturing process finds a place in the local community. Residual oils and sediment from processing tanks are taken to local organic dairy farmers because research shows that Omega-3 increases milk production.

1D businesses build walls that separate them from customers. 3D organizations, on the other hand, want to be part of their communities. Many of the 3D companies described in this book are leaders in their industry associations, as well as in their local community organizations. In 3D companies, working for customer success extends beyond actual customers to the communities where they live and do business.

Escaping the Machine

Employees in 3D companies feel like they have a connection to their internal and external communities, but there's something else, too – they feel more liberated to do their jobs in the best way possible. When I asked a customer service representative at Barlean's for a word she thought described the company's customer service culture, she said, "freedom." Real freedom is creative and proactive. It will take the organizational culture into new territories.

55

Employees join your company to take care of your customers. The organization must show them how to recognize the new viewpoint – the 3D perspective – and the level of creativity they can offer when acting on behalf of customers. Those accustomed to the increasingly out-dated command-and-control management style will be surprised to discover that they don't have to check with management to implement ideas designed to provide the level of service that gets customers talking – in a good way.

Companies can give basic 1D service without being customer-centered. There are plenty of books describing how to make employees more helpful, responsive and pleasant. To achieve 3D customer service, though, you need a system that begins with employees seeing their roles differently than they have in the past.

Customer-centricity requires employees who not only care deeply, but who are also encouraged to innovate for their customers. It can't be mandated, though – it needs to be cultural. Employees need to feel like they are contributing to building something that has a purpose. Organizations that want to be customer-centered monitor employee views about the freedom they have to add value to customers and to grow their relationships with them. Actions will be more customer-centered when employees are part of a culture that thinks like its customers.

The Multiplier Effect

In sports and music, the more you practice, the better you become. The same concept applies when creating a more customer-centered work environment. The more you do it, the better you get at it. In economics, this "multiplier" effect describes the degree of change in one variable that is caused by another.

That practice must be directed at the aspects of any performance that are most important to success. Unlike casual practice – hitting golf balls without studying how to improve, for example – deliberate practice can be challenging because it requires constant feedback and mental concentration. But it works.

Now transfer that concept to your business. If you're going to get better at something, shouldn't it be related to your customers? But deliberate practice is not automatically built into most organizations' work. It must be goal-oriented and structured to give us immediate feedback on how to improve our abilities rather than providing once-a-year feedback through annual performance reviews. Instead of using a short-term approach that follows one transaction with another, this type of deliberate practice in a business must have a long-term, organization-wide view. It must be driven by a feeling that you can always improve, a core belief that everyone must understand and own.

The opportunities are many, but creating this multiplier effect requires commitment. The journey begins by teaching the techniques used to think like a customer. But you won't get better at it unless you practice, so believe in the critical relationship of deliberate practice to extraordinary performance. Without a systematic approach, organizations are reduced to naively counting on customer excellence happening through individual transactions, rather than the exponential outcome produced by the multiplier effect. Great customer service performances don't come through individual deeds, but from a culture that believes in and practices customer-centricity.

MESA, an engineering, manufacturing and construction firm, has established the gold standard for customer performance with extremely high satisfaction scores in the cathodic protection industry, which hasn't been known for customer service. Yet, rather than accepting that as good enough, the company and its employees are using that momentum to continue to search for ways to outperform. A relatively new MESA employee, Sarfraz Shaikh, was surprised at the level of customer-focused teamwork. "Everywhere I went in the office, I saw banners describing how well-trained we need to be to effectively take care of our customers," he says. "There's a lot of cross-training so that employees learn all aspects of the business. I was impressed with the amount of information handed to people so that they can perform at a higher level for our customers."

There's another dimension of the multiplier effect that will add even more. While practice will help develop the skills for thinking like a customer, we can take that to the next level by praising remarkable performances. The multiplier effect translates into the motivation that sustains people through the challenges of getting better. It brings out their passion to serve customers.

57

Studies have demonstrated that students who were publicly identified as fast learners by their teachers or coaches were more motivated than average performers. We've all experienced this – reinforcement makes everyone believe in themselves (and their organization), so the motivation just happens. Praised performance generates more practice; the additional practice creates a better performance. You get the same results in the deliverables for your customers: Praised performances will motivate even higher customer focus. A small advantage is all that's needed at first. Tiger Woods, who started his golf training very early, received lots of positive feedback because he was not compared with more experienced players but with players his own age. That was his small advantage.

Success with customers, however, doesn't happen without careful nurturing. You don't just flip a switch and get passion. It requires communicating your successes throughout the organization, holding them up as models of customer-focused behavior. Document them as best practices so others can learn from them. The resulting passion will fuel unending new ideas that will drive higher brand loyalty in your customers. Motivation occurs throughout the organization when customer-centricity becomes preeminent, rather than something that employees have to "fit in" with their other duties.

Invest in the multiplier effect to catapult your business to the next level. Customer-centricity can become a reality if you encourage independence throughout your organization and praise superior customer performance when it happens. Great performers never allow themselves to operate on autopilot. They are always making a conscious effort to improve because they understand how powerful customer excellence can be when the multiplier effect is realized.

The Hiring Process

Great performers also need great people. The Strong, a Rochester, N.Y. museum, is both a collections-based facility devoted solely to play as well as an educational institution for the study and exploration of play. Families, children, adults, students, teachers, scholars, collectors, and others enjoy the National Museum of Play®, the National Toy Hall of Fame®, the International Center for the History of Electronic Games®, and other significant exhibits.

So the museum can provide the highest level of service possible for customers, Senior Vice President for Guest and Institutional Services Kathie Dengler starts by hiring "nice people" and training them to the organization's standards. The interview process includes walking through the museum to assess a candidate's level of enthusiasm about the surroundings. Once someone is hired, a formal mentoring program helps people develop professionally according to the museum's standards. Dengler believes that if an employee fails, the leader is to blame, not the employee.

The Strong refers to customers as guests and employees as hosts. The result, Dengler says, is that "We treat guests as we would guests in our home. We want the environment to be friendly, safe and clean."

Is there a specific gene necessary to be customer-centered? No, but it seems that way. At Barlean's Organic Oils, the high-performing customer-centered culture also starts with the hiring process. The company's goal is to build a healthier world and its employees are the spark for this possibility, so it looks for people with heart who have the potential for personal growth. CIO Jade Beutler notes that one of the "secrets" to Barlean's successful culture is hiring exceptional people who share the founders' philosophies about health, nutrition, quality products and service.

"We train for the principles, not the event," says Scott North, Barlean's director, customer services. "For example, when a bottle leaked on the other products in a shipment, we gave the customer credit for what was received in the order and gave them their next order free, too." He adds that employees are taught to treat their customers' money like it's their own. They discuss how they can do things better. "We talk a lot about examples with all employees to help them understand why we took the action we did," North adds. "Our leadership defines customer-centricity as 'everybody is your customer' and this feeling translates into a deeply personal attitude among employees."

Subscription management company cSubs begins its customer-centered cultural process by asking prospective employees a number of questions to determine whether candidates are capable of thinking like a customer. For example, interviewers describe a customer

59

problem and tell the candidate that none of the traditional solutions has worked before asking, "What would you do?" cSubs looks for people who are capable of developing out-of-the-box solutions.

Customer-Centric Managers

3D organizations need the right managers and leaders, too, especially because customer-centricity is cultural. But can middle managers transform a product-centric culture into a customer-centered one? Definitely.

Designing processes that add value to customers is an essential function of management. In 1D organizations, though, managers who might be customer-focused in principle often become disconnected from what they are supposed to be most knowledgeable about – their customers – because they're dealing with other issues. In contrast, the Customer 3D system promotes ownership of the customer by everyone, including middle managers. 3D organizations conduct regular meetings that connect theory with every day practice. Imagine how customer-centered your team will be if you lead them in weekly sessions designed to analyze actual performance and future opportunities that come from thinking like a customer. This shared workplace approach allows interpretation and legitimizes proactive, creative efforts by employees. It creates a mini-community of employees empowered to add value to customers and design new processes.

Customer-centric managers who are change agents must have:

1. Great communication among employees. This helps mobilize initiatives for the customer and celebrate victories.

2. A willingness to look for ways to add value to customers. If you think, "We make widgets and customers buy them," it's a huge leap to, "We are in the customer-value business and we just happen to sell widgets."

3. An ability to see how the needs of select groups of customers might differ from the needs of others. If, for example, your real estate company thinks the needs of a single 30-year-old woman who wants to sell her house are the same as a 65-year-old married couple, then your approach falls into the one-size-fits-all technique, which isn't 3D.

4. The capability to start a project without knowing what the end will be other than understanding that it will be better for the customer.

5. The passion to make sure that customers are aware of improvements as they're made.

6. The confidence to publicize the group's successes to executives and the rest of the organization, so that the transformation takes hold organization-wide.

A few passionate managers can change the culture in an organization by leading their team toward customer-centricity. As Intel's Andy Grove has said, "Nothing leads as well as example."[3] Executive leadership must set the tone and direction for customer-centricity. But middle managers are in the best position to know when to take off the training wheels and make change happen.

MESA's Sales Manager, Pat McDaris, told me, "It's personal. I want to make the customer's job easier. And that's what we try to do in all areas and at all levels of MESA. That's just who we are." That's the type of attitude more managers need to bring to work.

Getting Customers to Trust You
A well-trained workforce can help develop customer trust. We all talk about the importance of customer trust, but few organizations have a plan that anyone – executives or other employees – really understand. A solid trust-building plan includes specific practices that help people view performance through the lens of the customer along with a leadership that inspires employees to relate to those customers.

Building trust is similar to public speaking. Remember the truly awful presentations you've endured? The speakers were probably talking *at* you rather than *with* you. They were less concerned with you, and more concerned with advancing their own agendas. In situations like that, the speech becomes a chore for the audience instead of a positive, memorable experience.

Building customer trust, on the other hand, parallels the characteristics of a dynamic speaker. It starts with delivering a message on an equal-to-equal basis, which leads to energizing

61

conversations and the discovery of exciting new possibilities. It's a dialogue that goes beyond that monologue in which a company is lecturing the customer (the audience) about its products (the speech) and expecting them to buy in. The result is a harmonious and compelling relationship. Customers cease to be faceless and start to take an active part in the relationship. It's a matter of getting the information you need to understand their story and fitting your solutions to that story. Just as speakers must relate to their listeners, organizations need to connect with their customers. Organizations will perform better when they understand what it's like to be in the customer's world.

All great speakers create a better outcome for their audiences. 3D organizations have the same responsibility for their customers – to show them a new, different way they might not have visualized before. When this happens, a collective energy springs up because there's a different way of thinking. Customer 3D transforms individual work from a job to a purposeful career or a calling that employees can commit to.

Customer trust doesn't just happen. It has to be designed and cultivated. The formula for all successful speakers is to know their audiences and to adapt to audience needs. When they do that, they can deliver their messages in a meaningful way. It's a great lesson for an organization to learn on its journey to becoming customer-centered. The Customer 3D system helps your company develop the capability to anticipate the dynamic factors that determine how customers will react to the ideas and changes you are designing for them.

The Outside-In Mindset
Your customers, by definition, are outside the four walls of your organization. Progressive, successful organizations, however, look for opportunities to invite customers *in* to participate in internal activities. Why? Because 3D organizations respect their customers' intelligence. Since the Customer 3D system encourages smart perspectives from all directions, this outside-in mindset is a remarkable way to leave behind narrow, 1D behaviors and clearly validate customer-focus to all of your employees. It is also a way to

inject new ways of thinking into the organization. Clearly, it is easier to understand what constitutes "above and beyond" when the input of customers is immediate.

Examples include:

> To create value, leaders need to focus on connecting what goes on inside the firm with what goes on outside the firm-and act to connect the organization's programs to customers.
>
> *Dave Ulrich*

- A restaurant that invites customers to taste selections created by potential new chefs before they're hired.

- A manufacturing firm that asks customers to join the team that is defining competencies for first line supervisors.

- An organization that invites customers to interview potential new employees, before they are hired, to make sure the person hired is someone they could work with.

- An oil company invites customers to its in-house sales force training on new products. After customers participated with the sales staff in one training session, the region that did this outperformed a region that didn't by 10-to-1 in sales during the subsequent six months.

- A maker of heart valves has customers speak to employees after the surgery so that they grasp, in a more personal way, how their product saves lives.

Microsoft's Technology Center includes a Customer Immersion Center to give customers a more in-depth technology experience. The Center allows employees to observe how customers react to design features and to better understand the possibilities for productivity improvements. The office labs portion of the Center allows customers to tour and see the future concepts being developed. Microsoft uses feedback from these visits to improve customer experiences.

This is inclusion at its best, but sharing newsletters and other public communications helps transfer knowledge, too. Customers feel engaged and become advocates for your company in a way that transcends mere satisfaction. This approach represents more than simply connecting. It illustrates a belief that customers will find value in participating in your inside activities. Note, however, that

63

it doesn't give customers *the* voice, but *a* voice. It's based on the belief that customer participation will make your company stronger because customers will help you and your employees learn more about how to think like a customer. It's a low-cost investment that pays huge dividends in company culture and customer trust.

Why don't more organizations invite their customers into management corridors so everyone can benefit from the wisdom of those participants? In some cases, there's a sense that management knows "what's right," so this input isn't needed. In others, managers don't want to let go of any control. In still other situations, there could be a fear that customer influence will take them in a direction they don't want to go. Ironic, isn't it, that companies don't trust their customers, yet they expect their customers to trust them?

> Always do right. This will gratify some people and astonish the rest.
> *Mark Twain*

Managers in those scenarios can't see the upside – the enthusiasm of customers that will spread beyond the few allowed inside the four walls to others who simply enjoy the open attitude. It takes a confident, yet humble organization that wants to improve. These are the operations that will grow organically and continue to outperform their competition.

How many opportunities do you have to allow outside customers in to participate in your organization's advancement?

Do the Right Thing

People who are a good fit for 3D companies like working for organizations with an authentic "do the right thing" philosophy. WD-40, for example, believes that doing the right thing starts first with values. When CEO Garry Ridge was playing a round of golf at Pebble Beach, his caddy said to him "Right is right and wrong is wrong." It's really that simple, if the process is built from ethics and values that are well-understood and fundamental. The company once had a board member who people thought of as the perfect aunt. Everyone respected and looked up to her. Ridge said that doing the right thing equated to making decisions and taking actions with the thought of explaining them to her.

Perhaps you're a role model for recycling, giving back to the community, or encouraging volunteerism among employees. The lessons from this other-centered philosophy would undoubtedly carry over to your interactions with customers. It's possible to take it further, encouraging customers to support your more altruistic goals. But to be convincing, the options you present must appeal to them on economic, practical, and convenience levels. The goal is to create a rewarding and emotionally rich experience for customers, with alternatives they can choose from.

The essential element is designing your processes as a caretaker, with a focus on the future. With recycling, for example, you need to own the entire experience rather than rationalize that someone else should worry about what happens to the product or its packaging after you sell it. Success comes through encouraging customers, rather than by forcing or preaching.

This kind of caretaker connection can focus your work to improve any process within your company. Enlightened companies understand that thinking like a customer will help them develop products and processes which will, in turn, generate "automatic" relationships with those customers because these customer-focused systems make more sense. One success will jumpstart many others. What it will teach us, whether it's recycling or any other customer-facing process, is that it needs to be coherent and convincing, not naïve. The transformation is gradual, unfolding in stages. It's about creating the "next better thing" rather than perfection. And that in itself is a valuable lesson.

The new approach to customer-centricity embodies being a caretaker for the customer ecology in every interaction between external customers and your organization. The organizations that fall behind in the future will be the ones that fail to think creatively. They won't focus on designing an increasingly better outcome for their users. You can be different – harness your forces to design outcomes that will benefit both employees and customers, both individually and globally, and success will happen.

65

Athletes Use 3D Imaging. Professional sports teams and athletes are beginning to use motion capture technology to improve players' health and performance. This technology uses sophisticated sensors similar to those used for three-dimensional animations in movies such as "Avatar." These computer generated 3D models can ensure that athletes are not damaging their bodies through improper limb angles or stress on joints. The technology can also improve performance by indicating ways to increase throwing and running speeds to outperform the competition.

What if you assigned an impartial team with members who were knowledgeable of the elements of the Customer 3D system to "scan" your organization for details of processes that offered customer-centric opportunities? How many process improvements that would matter to your customers could be identified?

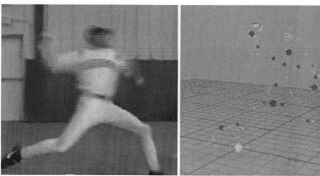

Figure 3.1

3D motion capture of Mariano Rivera; credit: Movement Lab at New York University

A Passion for Education

Employees of 3D organizations have a passion for educating their customers. They are always inventing new ways to make customer experiences more valuable. For example, South African Airways (SAA) focuses on improving performance by looking at each element of its service from the customer's viewpoint. It prints letters from customers in its in-flight magazine, which isn't unusual, but it answers each letter with a thank you note or letter mailed from an SAA employee. How do you think that makes the letter writer feel? Take that up a notch by responding to customers not only

66

with appreciation, but by showing how the company acted on their comments.

SAA believes in educating its passengers. A recent issue of the in-flight magazine explained how the autopilot mechanism works. What makes this remarkable is that SAA's employees were customer-focused to the point that they wanted to reassure passengers about how the autopilot function helps keep them safe. The airline also positions cameras on the tails of the plane so that passengers can see the entire plane and exterior during takeoff and landing, rather than just the runway, which is what some other airlines offer. As a result, South African Airways has won numerous airline awards. Organizations like this that outperform are always thinking like their customers. They are using their creativity while proactively asking customers about what they want to know and see, along with what they will appreciate. Customers really care about the attention that their service providers give them and become more engaged and committed as companies continue to give them things they never even asked for.

The organizations that will survive and thrive five years from now are the ones that have educated customers. That's because smart customers will remain loyal to suppliers that deliver high value. Fill in this blank for your organization: "An educated customer _____." If your answer is "will want a lower price" or "will look for a better product or service elsewhere," then you're living on borrowed time. Educated customers are not a bad thing – they're just the opposite. Customer-centered companies want to educate their customers because they know that these people will value the information, especially when no other supplier provides it.

Persuasion is a way of life these days. The best way to persuade customers to buy from you is to be proactive. Entice them first with your knowledge about your industry, then with your willingness to share that knowledge. If you want to be the market leader, show your customers that you are the expert they need. Be generous with your knowledge and you will create a community that is far superior to the traditional buyer-seller relationship.

Education is a significant component of customer relationship

67

building process at Barlean's Organic Oils. Barb Bloch loves this part of her job in customer service. "I like to be able to educate our customers and to relate to their health concerns," she says. "I answer the Brevail® line to answer questions about healthy breast tissue and help them with concerns with PMS and menopause. In my role, my number one goal is education."

To help shoppers select products that improve their health, the company provides retailers with helpful literature to offer in stores – even providing spinning display racks when necessary – and offers consumers a great deal of product and related information on the company's website. The consumer gets an education, the store gets credit for sharing the knowledge, and the company gets its name in front of its target customers.

Barlean's educates retailers, too, not only about its products, but about ways to be smarter retailers as well. For example, it hired a consultant to advise smaller retailers on how to become the "David's" of the classic David vs. Goliath retail scenario.

Educating your customers will help them understand your business better, especially since it's quite likely that many of them don't fully appreciate your value to them. That's not unusual – most companies have customers who aren't aware of the company's full portfolio and how they can use it to be more successful. When we did research for a client to verify this assertion on our part, our client used the findings as an opportunity to work more closely with its customers. It started that process with an education initiative.

Education helps expand your organization so that customers can see, know, and appreciate a fully developed 3D brand. When they appreciate your value proposition, they will become more loyal. And, an educated customer will tell others about your value, generating the best kind of marketing: good word of mouth.

Since a better life for customers is part of the purpose of 3D businesses, they are comfortable with sharing their knowledge with customers. Education becomes part of the company's value proposition, so customers will never want to leave them. When you are the customer, you want to be as informed as possible. Turn that idea around when you are the supplier. Think like a customer.

68

Inspiring Your Customers

What's better than educated, satisfied customers? Inspired customers.

Metroparks of the Toledo Area gets this. The organization's mission is to enhance the quality of life and inspire preservation efforts in this and future generations by providing a regional system of premier natural, historical, and cultural parklands maintained and operated to the highest professional standards. Yet customers might not always be thinking about the long-term benefits of preserving land. How, then, does Metroparks balance customer wishes with the mandate? By inspiring preservation in its customers.

It starts with a strong educational outreach to its constituency, but transcends to inspiration through consistent, passionate efforts of its staff members and their commitment to quality. For example, Metroparks offers a series of outdoor photography seminars at its National Center for Nature Photography at Secor Metropark. Local residents acquire a greater appreciation for the park's beauty while learning how to record and preserve nature's bounty.

Inspiring your customers has long-term benefits. It's like compound interest – it builds on its own growth. Inspired customers are enthusiastic, interactive and open to innovation. But you can't inspire unless you're thinking like a customer.

What Does "Wow" Mean?

Many times front-line employees are hampered by less-than-optimum systems and procedures that prevent them from delivering a customer experience that is intuitive. Or, if they offer ideas for improvement, management explains all the reasons that change can't happen. Isn't it disingenuous to tell front-line employees to go above-and-beyond when senior executives are missing the bigger picture?

A case in point is the frequent mandate to "wow" customers. There is certainly nothing wrong with the philosophy. You might use other words – delight, dazzle, amaze, etc.– but the overriding idea remains the same: to deliver a great experience. But what does "wow" really mean?

I had a conversation recently with a manager from one of my   69 suppliers, who shared with me that his corporate office wants his people to "wow" their customers. The problem is, this manager and others at the company aren't sure what this means because corporate hasn't really defined "wow" for them. Undoubtedly, without some guidance, the term can be interpreted in many ways and could vary depending on the needs of each customer. The employees are willing, but confused, because of the lack of direction.

In order for "wow" to work, it's important that everyone's on board with the concept, especially executives. Most often, senior management sends a message that, "We're going to keep everything in place from our product-centric environment – products, services, policies, procedures, inflexibility. But, by the way, in spite of these restrictions, make sure that you delight the customer." How can you win with those restrictions?

An authentic "wow" environment only happens when it's rooted in a strong, value-driven culture that permeates the organization. Zappos is legendary for its "wow" customer experiences, but the company has worked hard to develop this corporate-wide mindset. Its "10 core values," outlined in the company's *Culture Book* (get your copy at www.zapposinsights.com/main/culture-book/), include "deliver wow through service."[4] Employees can do that because of the freedom they enjoy to "be real and use your best judgment," another one of those 10 core values. The company goes even further, celebrating great service by telling the stories of "wow" experiences to everyone in the company. This is powerful. And it creates a happy workplace.

If you are going to make "wow" a verb, as Zappos does, change your culture from supplier-focused to customer-focused. When you do that, each employee will "wow" the customer because everyone will know what that means.

Re-passionize

Sometimes you need to create a word to describe something you really care about that hasn't been well-defined before.

I had the great fortune to meet a team leader in the service industry recently as her customer. She was the perfect combination of competence and enthusiasm. While she was serving me, she made recommendations about my purchase and made me feel very welcome by understanding my needs and providing suggestions that were just what I wanted. She used her knowledge to customize the solution that I ultimately purchased because she was able to get "on the same wavelength" and truly think like a customer instead of a seller. I experienced not only a fantastic experience, but a great conversation, as well.

She shared with me a word that she had created: Re-passionize. She uses that word when she trains her team. If it wasn't a word before, it is now. She uses it to help her co-workers refocus on serving their customers when the urgency of the job can cause them to lose sight of the people who are the real reason the organization is in business – customers. "Re-passionize" illustrates how she behaves with customers. It translates well for others who are attempting to be just as successful.

Isn't this the challenge that we all face just about every day? Thinking like a customer is the philosophy that grounds us in what is most important. It recharges the battery in our organization to deliver what our customers value.

As organizations grow, they forget the important stuff. 3D leaders spark a fire in their team by reminding them. It helps the entire organization intensify what it is doing for everyone it touches. It not only increases employee and customer satisfaction, but it also drives higher performance. Re-passionize!

A Culture that Clicks
It's fascinating to discover why some companies are so much more successful at relating to their customers than others. It has to do with the organizational culture and how employees have been educated to work together. A genuine focus on an "outside" common purpose, such as the success of customers, eliminates the silo mentalities that prevail in most product-centric companies. At Barlean's Organic Oils, for example, the entire company is focused on improving customer personal health and helping people reduce physical pain. All employees are working for a purpose – better health for their customers. Everyone is involved, not just a few.

71

The passion for the value that the company offers makes the employee involvement personal. At Barlean's, after Sarah Willett in customer service was encouraged during training to create her own title, she chose "ambassador." "I liked the ambassador title because I consider my role as an ambassador for health, like a UN ambassador," she says. "It's what I want to be held accountable for. It also creates lots of conversations with our clients and gives me a chance to talk with them about how our products can help improve consumers' health."

In *Click: The Magic of Instant Connections,*[5] the authors use the term personal elevation to describe the "gusto and energy" that result when people click together at an unusually high level. In these situations, the common bonds between people are so strong that they can "suspend the normal kinds of checks and balances that you might have in an enterprise." The book illustrates the concept with a study of string quartets. Although all the musicians at this elite level are talented, the biggest differentiator between successful and unsuccessful ensembles studied was the group dynamics of each. Those musicians that "clicked" outperformed the other groups, whose members didn't have a close rapport. The under-performing quartets were cordial, but seemed less cohesive and polished to audiences because each member had an individual interpretation for a given piece.

While this isn't surprising, it can still seem difficult, almost magical, to make this kind of interaction happen in a company. Within an organization, centering on customers and their needs transforms performances by overcoming any policies, procedures or territorial differences between employees or departments that could get in the way. When the core value of the organization rests on what is best for the customer, bickering suddenly disappears. The result is a culture in which employees are part of a group that has "clicked" by being customer-centered.

Create an Early Warning System

Being customer-centric will help you create an environment that lets employees develop great relationships with customers. That closeness with them will increase the speed with which you learn of changes that could impact your business. Customer-centricity, in other words, enables an early warning system – the capability to know customer needs more quickly than the rest of the market does.

In the 1990s, WEIDMANN Electrical Technology, Inc. a St. Johnsbury, VT, manufacturer of electrical insulation for transformers introduced VES, its Value Enhanced (Insulation) System. It uses a process optimization software tool that allows the company to perform a before-and-after cost comparison of the impact of its insulation design prototypes. It ultimately saves customers money by showing how new transformer designs need less insulation, copper, steel and other raw materials. Total dielectric clearance reduction has been averaging 20 percent over traditional models, but has gone as high as 30 percent.

"We know the market and have been successful in partnering with customers and helping their engineering departments," says Todd Thiele, vice president of sales. "We're doing what we're passionate about, and that has taken us from good to great." He notes that WEIDMANN's expertise far exceeds that of most clients or competitors. "We talk with customers about their needs and often become an extension of their engineering departments. This approach, which is part of our continuous improvement mentality, is a win-win for us and our customers. Because we reduce the required electrical clearances, we are able to reduce the size of a transformer by 5 to 7 percent. This lowers the cost and raises the efficiency at the same time," he adds.

Because WEIDMANN is so connected to its clients, it gets those early warning signals that make such a difference in an organization's success. Being customer-centered is the best way to position your business for that benefit. It will alert you to serious problems, providing strategists with time to anticipate, think and plan. In addition to getting important information early, you'll get better information, too. It's fashionable to say that we are in "the knowledge business," but if we're going to compete on knowledge, then it must be the best knowledge we can get. This goes far beyond a CRM (customer relationship management) system. Knowledge acquisition comes from a system designed to share customer know-how with everyone.

73

An organization that is customer-centric communicates with customers proactively, not reactively. To operate effectively, you must operate outside the four walls of your business. When you stay in tune with the latest information about customers and their needs, you won't be taken by surprise or caught off guard. "Fast" knowledge happens within organizations that are connected and proactively communicating with their customers. Every organization should have an early warning system. The best one is built around closeness with customers.

Rewarding Creativity and Entrepreneurship

Companies do not generate or develop energy in their customer relationships by serving – that's too passive. They build it by rewarding employee creativity. Customer-centricity works better when it is linked to the personality of the founders and company leaders. Customer-centricity becomes a core competency when it is strengthened and reinforced throughout the organization – not just imagined in an ivory tower.

At cSubs, the electronic subscription management company, President Julie Auslander's customer-focused leadership works at two levels. First, she encourages all employees, especially those who work directly with clients, to think like a business owner. "Each employee is empowered to act like me and to ask themselves 'What would Julie do?' with every customer," she says. Employees learn that customer work is not a transaction – it's a relationship. They are educated to understand the clients' personal lives and from this understanding to learn how to serve them better and more proactively.

Second, to create this team vision, she has created a program that rewards customer-centered behavior. The organization has identified 12 customer-centric behaviors that the organization wants all employees to model. They include identifying new clients and designing solutions that streamline processes for customers. The system attaches compensation to these positive behaviors, so employees earn points toward $5,000 vacations paid for by the company, as described in Chapter 2.

74 Auslander's leadership approach is intentional, not accidental. She

empowers her employees to think like an owner by encouraging them to serve customers with strategies that "feel right" rather than policies to follow without question. Andrea Buenaventura, a customer support representative, summarizes the work environment: "Because management treats people well, the company is rewarded by having loyal employees."

At Barlean's Organic Oils, employees are also given the opportunity to be creative. The entire company is receptive to entrepreneurial ideas; employees are free to explore them. At the same time, though, if the timing isn't right, management might say, "We like it, but it's not a top priority right now."

Great Performances

When you go to a show or event, you expect creativity and a great performance. What makes you think your customers don't expect that from you every day?

My wife and I attended a Second City comedy troupe show that included rehearsed sketches, improv, and a workshop in which the performers answered questions from the audience. When asked about how they handle "the same old" improv topic requests from the audience, a performer responded that they try to do it differently every time. While it would be easy to repeat jokes or scenarios that have worked successfully in the past, the cast member said, "I feel dirty if I don't deliver new material." He wants to give his customers – the audience – his best.

Contrast that attitude with another recent experience at a historical site in Salem, Mass. Our tour guide was knowledgeable, but bored – so he was boring. He covered the highlights during the last tour of the day, but covered them a little too quickly. He had probably done this tour hundreds of times before, but the Second City actors could probably make that claim, too, and that didn't seem to diminish their performance. The tour guide didn't seem to care very much about his audience. He wasn't thinking like a customer.

We are all performers on the job. While we might not be in the entertainment industry, we still need to approach our work with a willingness to give everything for the customer. Give good value

75

every time – value that's determined from the customer's viewpoint. This mentality is cultural and infectious. It's built from a sense of accomplishment when employees won't accept anything less than their best.

Barlean's helps employees by using a computer system that tracks responsiveness to customers. One of its goals is to give callers a live voice within 30 seconds. Employees are also able to see a progress report on the portal that's visible to the entire department. The system is updated twice a day with department performance and other key pieces of information. 99.9 percent of customer inquiries are handled on the first call because each of the customer service employees knows where to look for answers – and understands that customers value quick and friendly service.

Customer perceptions of a company are a cocktail of the people and processes they encounter. 3D employees deliver so well because they are allowed to be the expert. Every time they "perform," they know they will be successful if they think like their customers. They try to be fresh, creative and different from the last time they connected with those customers and to give them an extraordinary experience. After all, that's what customers appreciate – and it's what they will remember and talk about. When employees are mindful of the outcomes that customers value, they stretch their performance parameters and become 3D. They discover techniques or methods they didn't know were possible.

As companies grow, they often lose focus unless they "act small."A customer of cSubs volunteered that, "I know that they have other accounts, but I feel like I am their only customer. They are there instantly for me when I need them." When 3D organizations get that feedback about their culture, it's a great reminder of why they are in business.

Characteristics That Make 3D Organizations Legendary

3D organizations are fundamentally different from 1D businesses. 3D companies:

- Understand that being customer-centric requires an expanded focus. It is not continuing to operate as product-centric and simply behaving with better transactional courtesy toward customers
- Encourage employees to act as a family or tribe
- Makes decisions based on what is best for the customer rather than being constrained by a lot of rules and procedures
- Have strong leadership that drives the culture, but stays in the background by empowering employees
- Honor their customers rather than simply serving them
- Believe that everyone in the organization owns the customer, even if they aren't in customer-facing positions
- Educate customers about more broad-reaching, universal issues than the products that the company is selling
- Set a goal of showing customers how the company's products and services help those customers reach success
- Are organic, demonstrating wholeness, rather than fragmentation within their organizations
- Train for principles, not events.

PART II

You Say You Want a Revolution: How to Become 3D

Every generation needs a new revolution.
Thomas Jefferson

Customer 3D organizations have started a quiet revolution. Because they haven't been satisfied with the traditional, product-centered clichés about how to take care of customers, they have embarked on a journey to discover how to create a superior experience that customers will value.

They have focused on the traits that customers will remember them for:

- Simplicity
- Inspiration
- Education
- Added value

Customer 3D helps leaders' focus by asking this question: "How can I make life easier for my customers?" The answer will ultimately bring new customers to you while keeping current customers fantastically committed.

Chef Alice Waters describes her slow-food philosophy as "a delicious revolution." Her work is *inspired* by recipes, rather than

79

ruled by them. At the center of her approach is a need for good ingredients. In a similar way, 3D companies focus on using great ideas and highly motivated employees – their "good ingredients" – to deliver a "rich blend" of customer service flavors that sets them apart from the rest.

This broad-reaching revolution is beginning to re-shape companies that were confined by one-dimensional behaviors, but are ready to dust off the staleness and expand to a deeper, more exciting dimension.

Success in the future will not be about you. It will be about the other guy – the customer. The best customers – the customers you want – place a premium on innovation. 3D companies are constantly looking for different ideas and practices from all industries, not just their own. They build and re-combine them into more powerful hybrid solutions that benefit their customers.

In Part II, we will put a finer point on the 3D revolution with practical ways to make customer-centricity really sticky and ever-present in your organization. We will help you reflect on the image that your organization projects and to find your true voice, because that's how you will reach prospects and connect with customers. Customer 3D will lead you out of the past by creating the culture that's a better fit for the future. Remember, it's not what *your company* does, it's what *your customer* does that's important.

80

FOUR

Handle with TLC
(Thinking Like a Customer)

Thus, the task is not so much to see
what no one yet has seen,
but to think what nobody yet has thought
about that which everybody sees.
Arthur Schopenhauer

A revolutionary new dimension of leadership is emerging, one that resonates deeply with customers and leads to stronger loyalty. It places the organizations that practice it far above the average players in the eyes of customers. In addition, it is more sustainable because it's a unifying force for all activities within the corporate culture.

With this new organizational mindset, suppliers leave behind ordinary, conventional service and replace it with extraordinary performance. Customers become so captivated by this customer-centered originality that this new deliverable becomes their standard for performance from other suppliers.

Out-dated product-centric tactics – lowering prices and touting Six Sigma-driven internal efficiencies – create inertia and reactive decisions in companies that have ignored their customers. Consider the decades it took the auto industry to realize that old strategies and tactics would no longer solve its problems. The new environment requires proactive, value-added customer relationship ideas – and they're waiting to be developed in all industries. Organizations just need to design the right internal cultures.

81

One of the subconscious assumptions made by leaders of most organizations is that customers think like they do and want the same things they want. It's not true, and this assumption can be a detriment to success. Old assumptions need to be replaced with the new "thinking like a customer" approach. The TLC acronym stands not only for "thinking like a customer," but also that old standby, "tender loving care." We give tender loving care to things that are valuable and irreplaceable – family members, heirlooms, expensive investments. Our customers need the same kind of care. It's a great reminder of not only how valuable our customers are to us, but also of the mindset we must maintain to understand our organizations and the way customers think about them.

The essence of an organization that is customer-centered is its willingness to think like its customers. When companies focus on customer solutions, their range of vision opens up and they begin looking for opportunities that were there all along, but went unnoticed. "Old" customer basics are one-dimensional and no longer effective. If you want to think like a customer, think in three dimensions.

Reactive Thinking

Product-centric thinking is based on the one-dimensional view that a company's products or services are all that is necessary in order for customers to be happy. The organization exists simply to supply that product to the customer and every customer experience is viewed as a transaction. Figure 4.1 illustrates the separation between this transactional mindset and a customer-centered, proactive, 3D organizational approach. The one-dimensional, product-centered portion of the illustration describes the performance of organizations in everyday transactions or touch points with customers. It's necessary for survival, of course, but not sufficient for growth.

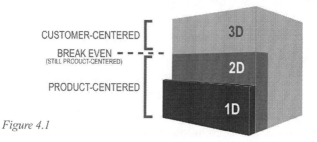

82   *Figure 4.1*

Organizations operating at this level take care of under-served customers by handling orders according to policies and procedures and resolve customer problems when they arise.

Organizations with a product focus evaluate their performance for customers predominantly in this first dimension. It's what most people mean when they refer to "customer service." Companies assess how well they do largely on how their products and services perform, how employees handle encounters with customers, and how they solve customer problems. Although this is important, it represents "table stakes" – the expectation to get into the game.

When this one-dimensional world goes well, it is primarily defined by what happens when an employee delivers "good" service (friendly, helpful, etc.) during a typical buyer-seller encounter. If you have a satisfactory experience during a transaction with your supplier, but the employee that took care of you was energetic and courteous, this result can be called two-dimensional (2D), This experience is better, of course, but it is still traditional and ordinary. It is simply a product-centered mindset with a great delivery by individual employees. If we aren't mindful that there is something better, it's easy to become immune to customers' experiences and fall into a rut, believing that this basic, courteous, service is the only thing needed. 1D and 2D friendly performances can be referred to as "looking *at* your customers." You aren't ignoring them, but you're looking at them through your "supplier" eyes. This is the prototype of product-centric behavior. Although it is appreciated by customers, it is still expected and very ordinary in today's world.

Organizational success depends on how companies define customer needs. If they think only in terms of 1D transactions, that's all they'll get – 1D service. There's also the danger of functional silos developing because customer ownership isn't defined, or employees make judgments based only on their department outputs. Companies with this mindset primarily think in terms of a system that pushes goods and services toward the customer. They aren't aware that anything's missing.

Product-centric leaders in 1D companies think their responsibility is to eliminate customer problems – to get the customer to even, as

83

noted in Figure 4.1. The 3D vision, on the other hand, is developed around "abundance," so its practitioners are always looking for ways to proactively help the customer. The focus of 3D organizations is to go beyond break-even to a level where they are continuously designing new opportunities that benefit customers. When you are a customer, don't you want your supplier to deliver a 3D performance?

Have you ever had a perfectly adequate customer service experience that just left you flat? The transaction was adequate and the person serving you was pleasant and competent, but there was nothing special about it. That piece you sensed was missing inhabits the territory we call 3D. Breakthrough activities for genuine, world-class customer-centricity happen only in the third dimension. It involves proactively delivering abundant, extraordinary performances that go far beyond customers' wants and expectations.

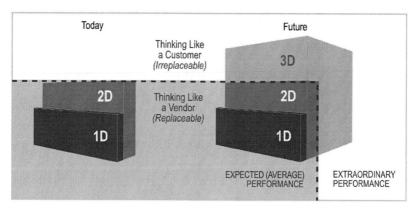

Figure 4.2

Look at the diagram in Figure 4.2. The majority of organizations operate only in the 1D-2D territory because they believe that is all that customers expect. Customer 3D companies have their share of transactional actions that must be handled, of course. However, they think outside the 1D-2D dimension to elevate their culture. What if organizations empowered employees to make purposeful customer decisions which looked far beyond a transactional mindset? Imagine not seeing 2D as a stopping point which considered delivering product plus courtesy as "enough" for the customer, always operating above the line that designates expected service. That is where 3D organizations operate – making them exceptional. That

84

is how 3D organizations drive stronger customer loyalty and brand commitment. That's where TLC can take your organization.

1D – 2D – 3D Behaviors

What do customers experience when working with highly engaged 3D companies? Let's explore some examples of how a Customer 3D culture outperforms 1D and 2D behaviors toward customers.

Scenario #1: A customer is buying a gallon of paint at a "big box" retailer. Following is what could be expected from the three dimensions of organizational culture:

- 1D. Employees narrowly view their job simply to mix and sell the paint to the customer.
- 2D. The employee asks how the customer will be using the paint in order to ensure the proper product is provided for the solution that the customer needs. He or she shows concern for the needs of the customer.
- 3D. The organization captures the learning from the customer and communicates it as a universal "best practice" that will help other employees and other facilities. It creates a system to make more knowledge available to other employees so that they do not have to "reinvent the wheel." It also uses storytelling to legitimize the actions taken on behalf of the customers and models this behavior (and outcome) for employees which strengthens the culture and which, in turn, creates more value across the organization by leading to the same or similar consultative roles provided to ALL customers.

1D organizations want to minimize the efforts they put forth for the customer. Rules and procedures that the customer must follow tend to help keep this effort down because if customers ask for exceptions, these requests can be deterred with "policies" that prevent saying 'Yes.' 3D is a whole new category of customer closeness. It is not product-centricity with a little courtesy added. 3D organizations are consultative.

Scenario #2: Patients are being admitted to the Emergency Room facility at a local hospital. The healthcare facility is backlogged, crowded, and waiting times are several hours.

- 1D. Questions from patients are routinely answered with responses about what hospital procedures say and individual

85

requests are turned down because exceptions cannot be made. The dignity of customers (patients) is approached from a "lowest common denominator" philosophy in order to treat everyone equally. The organization is focused on its equipment and metrics such as patient survey scores, total revenue, accounts receivable and staff turnover rates.

- 2D. The healthcare facility develops a reputation for being friendly and professional in the carrying out of its established procedures. Wait times are explained and expectations are clearly defined for the customer. Metaphorically, they have "polished the doorknobs" but the doorknobs have not changed.

- 3D. All functional areas are aligned and going in the same direction toward patient success because they understand that what happens for the customer goes beyond individual actions. Leadership reinforces that the common purpose of the organization is to go beyond a simple "absence of illness" state to one in which everyone is working for patient health and vitality long-term. Employees, including physicians, are trained to question each customer's experience in the facility by whether it 'makes sense' to the customer and they are empowered to make proactive decisions by anticipating customer needs that are not being met completely. There is strong communication of best practices when they occur so that the culture is empowered to build on them with even more ideas.
Employees advocate for improvement ideas based on how they will benefit customers. When ideas require formal changes to systems and procedures, there is an ideation process which evaluates opportunities quickly and either deploys these ideas or provides feedback to the originators about why they cannot happen.

Employees throughout 3D organizations love what they are doing. The executive leadership invests in systematic approaches for creating a positive customer-centered culture throughout the organization. 3D healthcare organizations know that innovation in their systematic processes, based on patient-centered excellence, will take performance to a new dimension that 1D organizations are only chasing. Executive leadership understands that improving patient outcomes will require first investing in and focusing on the culture of the organization itself. Building on this culture initiates the positive results and the company begins to outperform its competition.

1D businesses are programmed to behave in an ordinary way. 3D organizations behave in a role-model way. They know that by focusing on patients (customers), that their market share and patient satisfaction and loyalty will increase and their error-rates, staff turnover and accounts receivable days will go down as they expand to this new dimension.

Scenario #3: A consumer purchased a set of kitchen knives from a manufacturer with a full replacement policy if any of the knives is no longer functional. When one of the knives breaks, she returns it to the supplier, with an explanation required by the manufacturer's policy, in order to receive the replacement knife. The three dimensions would respond very differently when the request is submitted:

- 1D. The company ships the replacement knife to the customer at no charge. Employees process the documentation necessary to replace the knife and return it to the consumer. Employees have been conditioned to follow procedures that are in place without variation because if systems are "automatic" they will be more efficient. Protections are in place to prevent consumers from cheating the system for merchandise that they don't deserve.

- 2D. The company ships the replacement knife with an apology note and a company catalog showing other knifes that have been added to the line since the customer's knife was originally purchased. However, the company's response is still reactive rather than proactive.

- 3D. The company makes the return process more intuitive. It gives the customer credit for what she had (no returns were necessary) and enlists the consumer's help in making the products and services that we offer even better. Employees don't use the word 'policy' with customers. They are educated to ask "How can we do this better?" and to proactively take care of the knife replacement process with customer-centered ideas to stay ahead of the curve. They are encouraged to come up with fresh approaches that reflect the company's values. They can implement creative ideas: "What can we do to make the customer tell his or her friends about the replacement system that we have?" "How can we use her story on the company website and demonstrate to other customers what the company cares about?" There is a spirit of unselfishness, focused on higher performance rather than selling more. The selling will come later.

87

1D organizations share many common traits. They have a fear of losing control. They have a lack of trust in their employees. They have a limited mentality, resulting in the attitude that, if it is "different," let's restrict it. 3D organizations, on the other hand, share a frustration with things that are not user-friendly and they feel ownership for making these processes more customer-centered. They have developed the capability to see the thousands of touch-points with their customers as opportunities to improve by thinking like a customer.

Risk is a strong consideration behind the decision-making of 1D organizations. These are companies that have trouble maintaining their competitive advantage, leading to inertia, complacency, and the commoditization of their products. The dynamic between a corporation and its customers used to be us-versus-them and success in these times carried with it some arrogance – where the supplier thought it was more important than the customer. Today, that has all changed. It is getting difficult to differentiate your products (for longer than six months) because they are easily copied. The new competitive advantage is in lowering risk through customer closeness and greater trust. 3D companies have created a culture in which employees consult with customers – not because they have to, but because they want to do it.

A New Vision

Because customers see their suppliers as complete organizations, customers judge vendors by their overall perception of the relationship rather than by the outcome of individual transactions. When purchasing an automobile, for example, customers don't simply rate the car dealer's performance by whether they liked a car and got a fair price. They take much more into account – how they were treated, whether the experience was pleasant or painful, if dealership hours were convenient, and so on. Customer perceptions develop out of a complex system comprised of hundreds of obvious details as well as more subtle points that they observe and absorb during the course of the purchase process.

When a company delivers a flat, one-dimensional performance, customers become frustrated. It's not simply because the transaction might have gone poorly, but because the customers get the

88

impression that the entire company is one-dimensional. Over time, they use their collective experiences to make judgments based on the quality and culture of organizations with which they interact.

It's up to the leaders of those organizations to define what that image is going to be. Will it be a one-dimensional façade, or will it be 3D – organic and full of life?

> The difficulty lies, not in the new ideas, but in escaping from the old ones.
> *John Maynard Keynes*

All organizations should have a clean, clear vision of how they look to their customers – a 3D version that includes every aspect of the relationship, from product quality and transactional courtesy to how focused the culture is on customer success. If they aspire to be customer-centered, they must fully comprehend how they really look to those customers. If they want to be proactive, for example, then they need to truly "look" proactive at all layers within their organizations. Only with this full understanding can they be aware of the tweaks that are needed to design a system for continuous improvement.

3D organizations have this new solution-based insight, viewed from the new perspective is that of the customer. Inside the organization it becomes contagious. Employees are more committed to the corporate mission and purpose. Therefore, they put real energy into their work because they understand that, by seeing their actions from this new perspective, that the customer completes the work they are doing.

- 1D is transactional. However, organizations that are only focused on the transaction are underperforming for their customers. What they are doing is not WRONG, but there is more out there to be done. They have not realized their full potential. Companies that are product-centric are focused only on what is best for them. These 1D companies believe that if they eliminate problems--if everything "works" to a standard--that the customer will be satisfied. However, more and more, customers want something better.

- 2D is still transactional, but employees are courteous and thoughtful and care about making the customer experience smooth during the transaction that they are dealing with. However, it is still dominated by a break-even mindset. 2D companies narrowly believe that if the customer has no

89

problems (defined from the supplier's viewpoint) and the supplier's employees are friendly and professional, what else can the customer want?

- 3D is iconic. It's not a series of superficial changes; it's a different way of thinking using a deliberate, vision-focused approach. It consists of employees that are able to recognize a new, different, and more promising story that they could be delivering to customers, which they have not visualized up until now. It is epitomized by a new culture that consistently questions how it can improve, even if the customer has not asked for anything better. 1D organizations are concerned with keeping their feet on the floor, whereas 3D companies are reaching for a higher vision that will connect them with the customer even more than today. In 3D businesses, innovation is not just a journey; it's a workout, because thinking like a customer never stands still.

Being customer-centric is transformational. It is a systematic practice focused on great performances that are institutionalized rather than done transactionally. In addition, 3D organizations invest in developing and sustaining this customer-centered culture and have, therefore, raised their effectiveness across the entire culture. Because it creates a collective energy, which is greater than the sum of its parts, Customer 3D improves the supplier's performance as much as it pleases the customer. The Customer 3D system allows organizations to show employees what their customer-centered future will look like. And it empowers employees with the ability to create the future on the organization's terms, which are really their customers' terms.

Customer-Centric Problem Handling

There are differences in how 1D, 2D and 3D organizations handle problems, as well. While traditional, product-centered companies believe that all they need to worry about is eliminating customer problems, 3D companies enable their customers to succeed by visualizing customer service that always evolves. 3D leaders educate employees to believe that the organization will attract more and more loyalty by doing – and being – what customers want.

Customer-centric companies don't deliver perfect performance for their customers every time. But they handle shortfalls much differently than supplier-centric organizations do. Virtually every

1D customer service book talks about how an organization must have a process in place to recover (in the eyes of the customer) from service problems or missteps. But it's not enough anymore. Today's customers want something better.

The typical prescription in these cases focuses only on the problem and how to get the customer back to even (the absence of a problem). There's an apology and perhaps an offer of some sort of compensation. In today's business environment, this break-even direction is expected – it's the minimum behavior. What's better is using the problem to begin building an abundant relationship with the customer.

When I stayed in a hotel in Johannesburg recently, it had only been open for five weeks. There were a lot of problems to work out. But the staff took care of problems as they arose, and after the manager got me back to "even," he continued to build our relationship by providing exceptional, personalized service. He used my name in face-to-face greetings and regularly followed-up to make sure things had improved. I felt like I was his favorite customer – ever. I not only forgot about the earlier problems, I also felt great about the entire three-day experience.

Service recovery means staying with that customer through follow-up and, later, through unexpected contact. We should deliver exceptional service to all of our customers, of course, but the customers who have endured a less than ideal service performance represent a touch point that defines an organization. This is an opportunity to turn them into enthusiasts and maybe even evangelists. It's accomplished by inhabiting the customer's mind, so to speak. It goes far beyond a break-even reaction to the problem to, instead, anticipating how that event can and should happen in the future. It involves a willingness to work for that change.

Our client research shows us time and time again that customers who reported a problem and were delighted with the outcome have higher satisfaction than those who never experienced a problem at all. Why would any company only want to break-even with these opportunities? Service recovery should energize the organization to become more customer-centered, putting demands on our imagination. It should trigger that vision that makes us think

91

about how we can create customer service that's better than ever. Customer-centered organizations always work toward abundance, innovating with creative solutions to delight customers.

Abundance Gaps

The phrases "delight our customers" or "wow our clients" have been tossed around long enough. Frankly, most companies that say this are probably not delivering with action that makes a real difference for customers. More importantly, employees have difficulty understanding what this means. On the other hand, by defining great customer service as "abundant," organizations know to think creatively and innovate with ideas that have never been implemented before.

"Abundance," in this context, means that companies believe that there is a lot more to give to their customers than the minimum it takes to keep their business. When the organization's litmus test is "What would the customer think?", they have a system for delivering products and services in a new form. It's one that customers haven't seen before, but one that they value. "Abundance" is the new model for serving customers.

Successful organizations that focus their efforts on enabling abundance understand that the way to win and keep customers is to always anticipate how those customers want to receive their product or service. They have taken the quantum leap from thinking that all customers want is a lack of problems to educating employees that only extraordinary performance in serving customers is acceptable.

During training sessions for hosts at The Strong, the Rochester, N.Y. organization that is home to the National Museum of Play, leaders take real situations that have occurred in the museum and see how employees would react. Kathie Dengler, senior vice president for guest and institutional services, says, "We educate them to believe that there is more than one way to solve a problem. We also support our staff when they make a decision. In order to know that they are empowered, they have to know that we will support them." Taking this education process even further, The Strong trains the staff at the privately owned in-museum restaurant, too, so that they meet the same standards as the museum's employees. This commitment to employee education is so powerful because it leads to continuous improvement.

When companies believe that eliminating problems will keep the customer satisfied, they're supporting a philosophy that's narrowly focused on eliminating negatives from the customer's perception of an organization's performance. Using a healthcare example, this is the equivalent of moving from being sick to not being sick anymore. From a business standpoint, this is a move from problem-laden and inefficient performance to average efficiency and reliability.

A gap in an organization's abundance represents the difference between a state of "no problems" to one where performance is exceptional. Using that same healthcare example, closing this gap means moving from a lack of illness to absolute vitality. From a business standpoint, this is a move from average effectiveness to excellence. Organizations that can close these abundance gaps really win the hearts and minds of their customers. Customers are not only satisfied, but they keep coming back because they want the flawless performance that only these organizations can provide. They want to have a relationship with suppliers that think the way they do.

Most organizations give lip service to being solutions-providers to their customers. But when they proactively think like their customers, they create an energy source that attracts even more customers, just as the sun attracts plants. Instead of simply being a one-dimensional provider of goods or services, these organizations are the center of an ecosystem that delivers what customers need to be successful.

Proactive Solutions for Customers

Proactive thinking lets organizations extend their customer connections beyond basic 1D traditional service. Customer 3D is based on the belief that providing services and options that customers haven't even asked for will galvanize the organization in ways that generate better performances. Customers aren't always able to communicate everything they need. They don't know how to articulate these "silent" needs specifically, but they can sense them. 3D organizations learn how to pay attention, even when customers

93

aren't actually saying they have a problem, so that they can anticipate these silent needs.

The Strong focuses on anticipating the needs of customers. Museum employees are taught to pay attention to guests so they can provide what's needed when it's needed. For example, they understand that senior citizens have different needs from other customers – young children or even the parents of those youngsters – so they make it possible for seniors to take breaks in chairs with arms that make it easier to get up, have a cup of coffee, or visit with people who have similar interests. The museum helps make sure they get what they need.

> The intuitive mind is a sacred gift and the rational mind is a faithful servant. We have created a society that honors the servant and has forgotten the gift.
>
> *Albert Einstein*

The more expansive Customer 3D system delivers services for customers that develop from an organizational culture like The Strong's that's committed to differentiating customer performance so it stands out from competitors. It's a new, creative mindset – one that views everything involved with customer connections as a system rather than a sum of individual transactions. Organizations with an organic system in place continuously improve their products and services by pulling customer needs in, owning those needs, and taking care of them.

At this stage, organizations have created a system that hones their ability to be completely attentive to customers. It might involve solutions to processes or products that already exist in one form, but which can be improved to make them more customer-focused. Or, it could encourage behaviors geared to inventing new products and services that are focused on making life easier for customers.

Nick Collison, director of e-content and procurement support at subscription management company cSubs, says it equates to relationship management – understanding what the customer needs and delivering it. "We have to have a pro-active view in serving the customer," he says. "We recently had a client in the accounting field that needed an academic article. We located it from a vendor in

94

the UK. However, when the recipient opened the PDF document, it wasn't what he wanted, so we didn't charge him."

cSubs continually looks for solutions to problems before clients even know they're problems. For example, it regularly reviews client order lists to identify multiple copies of a publication so it can notify the customer in case they want to reduce the number by encouraging sharing.

In addition, employees are always thinking of ways to improve and streamline work flows. For example, when one employee couldn't process credit card orders quickly enough because of her workload, a colleague suggested that others help her for two hours daily until she was caught up.

A 3D structure and attitude makes it possible to design products and processes that are simpler and more intuitive for customers – proactively offering solutions before they're requested, as cSubs does. The moving walkways in airports are another example of how this works. While passengers using them still have to walk from Point A to Point B, it's a lot easier and faster with the moving walkways than without them.

Similarly, automobile gas gauges once simply indicated gas tank levels from empty to full. Later, manufacturers introduced the gas pump icon on the gauge for easier identification. Now, the identification process has progressed to include a triangle indicating the side of the car where the gas cap is located. This evolution has created a display that is more convenient and more intuitive for drivers. It's a good illustration of the thousands of creative 3D ideas in every business just waiting to be implemented.

Every process can be improved. Remember when guests provided their names to the hostess at busy restaurants, then had to wait nearby to hear their names called? That process became more dignified when restaurants began giving guests an electronic device that buzzes, lights up, or vibrates when their table is ready. Some restaurants are even sending text messages to waiting guests when it's time to seat them. What do you think should be the next evolution in this sequence?   95

3D Express Bus in China. China has developed an innovative system in which city buses can drive over cars by straddling them. The "three-dimensional fast bus" will reduce pollution and relieve congestion without widening roads. It ultimately will represent a win-win outcome and will increase the capacity of the roadway by moving the bus vertically while allowing passenger cars to travel under it in a tunnel effect.

How can your organization use thinking like a customer to revise a process in order to remove a bottleneck and, in turn, to deliver a faster response to customers while the process is carried out behind the scenes (i.e. not noticed by customers)?

Figure 4.3

Proposed by Shenzhen Hashi Future Parking Equipment Co., Ltd Photos: China news

Amplitude

3D organization leaders know that their companies can be measured by their "amplitude," which refers to the fullness that is created when the cultural shift is made. This critical dimension is used by sensory-analysis experts to describe food flavors that are blended and balanced. The best-tasting food brands have high amplitude. We all recognize the superiority, for example, of a gourmet chocolate chip cookie when compared with packaged off-the-shelf brands offered in a supermarket.

In a 3D organization, this amplitude – this wholeness – happens when all of the internal elements converge and are centered on the customer. Just as we can identify the difference between the tastes of top cola brands Coca-Cola and Pepsi when compared with private-label colas, we can understand the difference in organizations that connect extremely well with their customers. The amplitude manifests itself as a balance or blend in an outcome that's superior to the rest of the market, one that customers can clearly recognize.

96   High amplitude is the destination of the 3D journey. Successful

companies have a standard of excellence that they never compromise. The secret, however, is not in products and marketing. The secret is in creating this excellence from the viewpoint of the customer, because that is who will ultimately be the judge of whether that high status is deserved.

The Third Dimension and Customer Purpose

Amplitude applies to how well an organization provides better solutions to customers. The Customer 3D system embodies a solutions approach that's based on what customers want, not what the company sells. It's a superior approach because it involves evaluating every touch point in processes to look for improvements that the customer will notice and appreciate.

This engrained process of "thinking about what no one has thought about, but what everybody sees" is the essence of Customer 3D behavior. It leads organizations to rise above complacency with everyday experiences. It is strategic, because working in this new dimension produces a new reality for customers.

> It is not our purpose to become each other; it is to recognize each other, to learn to see the other and honor him for what he is.
>
> *Hermann Hesse*

That 3D attentiveness to the customer, like design, contains "the energy of its maker." It generates success because it embraces the philosophy that the customer "completes" the work we're doing. Naturally, when organizations think this way, they heighten customer loyalty because this new approach is one that customers might not have encountered before.

Customer 3D unleashes an ability to learn through experience in a way that generates a fresh, attentive view of how our products and services impact our customers. This paradigm shift brings one other very important element into play: a unifying structure. Organizations that operate at the 3D level have a positive, customer-centric culture that rises above the perception of customer transactions as fragments of a whole. The three-dimensional result is a wholeness that the customer experiences and values.

There's a renaissance happening, one that's shifting organizations so that they think like customers. They are filling the gap between

97

engineering and marketing with independent thinkers who are able to design solutions viewed through the lens of the customers.

A growing number of 3D success stories are helping us understand that being customer-centered is the best way to generate positive change in an organization. Many people hate change because it's foisted on them. They didn't ask for it; they don't believe it makes their lives easier. What happens, though, if we view change as an opportunity rather than as interference with "business as usual?" What if we develop a culture that aggressively asks, "How we can make this better for the customer?" What if change develops because of that attitude? The payback can be enormous.

In building stronger customer connections, 3D organizations ensure that employees are as close to customers' ways of thinking as possible. They build a business on better information, processes, and insight into what customers need to make it easier for them to engage with the organization. This kind of customer-centered change brings with it trust from those customers – and that should be every organization's primary goal.

In another case of developing new services, cSubs created a purchasing platform for a client that allows its customers to purchase directly from the client's site. Nick Collison, business development manager, says, "We served as the intermediary between the business and purchasing, helping the client on their market-based needs." cSubs also customized another client's dynamic and constantly changing subscription "catalog" so that the structure is much more user-friendly.

Customers embrace innovations that make life easier – that's what makes them "sticky." Customers don't want product-centric ideas pushed on them – they want their experiences to become better and better. That's where your change initiatives must be focused.

Ready for Peak Performance

One of the challenges with innovation and growth is making certain you can handle the positive outcomes that come with both. It's important, then, to make sure you anticipate customer needs when your system is in highest demand so that your performance will not falter when you're at your busiest.

I had the misfortune of spending two days in Reagan National Airport, courtesy of US Airways. I had a confirmed ticket, but the airline was seriously oversold because it was trying to accommodate some of the fliers from more than a thousand flights cancelled by a competitor. Anyone who travels frequently is bound to encounter these types of delays and problems. The essential issue, however, was that US Airways couldn't handle the volume of problems. Any organization, not just an airline, must have a system in place to handle a significant increase in business volume. If you can handle only a standard volume of changes in your business, you will fail when the number of exceptions increases.

Barlean's is consistently trying to take the burden off its customers. Scott North, director of customer service, lists a number of different ways that his company makes life easier for customers, including:

1. We anticipate their needs based on their buying pattern and, if they forget to order, we call them, but we never force them to place orders.
2. Customers are notified if UPS has damaged their shipment en route so that a replacement order can be processed.
3. Customers don't have to file any freight claims.

There is one other benefit of this common-sense, proactive operational planning. Barlean's can maintain enough product inventory to eliminate running out. As a result, it prints everything on invoice paper when it ships, rather than order acknowledgements followed by invoices as a separate transaction. Practical thinking about what the customer needs, therefore, creates efficiencies for the company, too.

"We are a destination-driven product," says North. "We have more product in stock than others. If an order is placed on Monday, it ships on Tuesday and arrives by Thursday." The company also lets customers, retailers and consumers create an "auto-ship" account to automatically replenish their supplies. This straightforward system was showcased in the book, *Strategic Supply Chain Management*.[1]

Every organization performs these day-to-day transactions, of course.   99

However, 1D companies often struggle with getting them done accurately. 3D businesses, on the other hand, know that when good processes resulting from smart planning are in place, the system is resilient and can withstand higher volume. If they aren't in place, chaos ensues. Within 3D organizations, 1D performance is effortless. The time and decision-making for the 1D issues amounts to almost nothing. Customers relate to organizations that share this generative, idea-developing energy with their customers. Consequently, these suppliers are perceived as higher performers. They are legendary, rather than ordinary.

When a supermarket knows it will have higher volume than usual – when a winter storm is predicted or just before Christmas – they add more cashiers because of the anticipated high demand. Customers judge your business by how you operate during these high volume situations. Every successful organization builds in more than enough capacity to handle these exceptional times. In doing so, they minimize the turbulence for customers by using systems that are logical and effective when viewed through the lens of those customers. A company has to be able to behave normally in abnormal situations.

The Seventh Hat

But how does an organization figure out how to build in that extra capacity for high-volume situations? Sometimes, it's about creative thinking. Edward de Bono is renowned for his groundbreaking work in lateral thinking and systems for generating ideas. In his book, *Six Thinking Hats*[2], he describes a technique for "channeling" thoughts about a problem or improvement opportunity by putting on one of six hats. It is a solid, proven technique that asks decision-makers to adapt one point of view at a time:

- White hat for facts and figures
- Red hat for emotions and hunches
- Black hat for caution and possible difficulties
- Yellow hat for positive speculation and benefits
- Green hat for provocative, creative thinking
- Blue hat for control and monitoring

He calls these hats "direction labels for thinking." They take participants in up to six different directions to look for answers and alternatives. Building on the cliché, "put on your thinking cap," he challenges us to maximize the brain's sensitivity in different directions.

The process of becoming Customer 3D provides a parallel approach, in which change-makers think like a customer. de Bono has pointed out how thinking, in general, can become confusing when we attempt to think too broadly at once. We need a more narrow focus. At the same time, for us, the risk of six-hat thinking is that it can focus on the supplier's viewpoint only, even if approached from six directions. 3D thinking requires focusing on those six areas as well as what will improve your product or service for the customer. This added effort – this need to think like a customer, too –is a seventh hat. Put on that hat and explore what the customer will value and how you can design a system or process for it.

We can all get better at looking through the eyes of customers to define how each decision we make will provide greater value to them. It takes practice. It also requires eliminating the clutter that distracts us. When done properly and consistently within your company – with seven hats – it becomes the cornerstone of actionable decision-making that everyone can understand and rally around. The 1D approach amounts to looking into the eyes of your customers. 3D organizations, on the other hand, look through the eyes of their customers.

Customers Need to Feel Comfortable
My wife and I were in a casino recently playing the slot machines for fun (certainly not for profit!). When we cashed out, the machines gave us bar-coded receipts with the dollar totals that we could use throughout the establishment. Interestingly, as the receipts were printing, the machine made the sound of coins hitting a metal catch bin. How clever was that? I smiled when I heard the non-existent coins dropping into the bin. I knew they weren't really there, of course, but the sound made my experience more fun. That manufacturer gets a lot of credit from me for showing such creativity.

There's a word for this little "device" that made me smile. It's "skeuomorph" and it's defined as a design feature copied from a similar object in another material, even if it's not functionally necessary. As products evolve, it's important for designers to ensure that customers are comfortable with the difference and accept the new feature or technology as a logical improvement rather than a drastic change. In the case of the slot machine, keeping a feature that gamblers are accustomed to – the sound of coins dropping on metal – helps them adapt to the new process and even amuses them.

There are more skeuomorph examples than you might expect. They reflect the willingness of the designer and manufacturer to consider the customer's need to feel comfortable with new configurations and technology:

- A copper-colored U.S. penny, even though the coins are made from a zinc alloy and contain no copper
- The clicking sound of a digital camera, imitating film moving forward and indicating that the picture has been taken
- Wood finish on a plastic product
- Denim jeans with non-functional rivets
- Metered postage showing wavy lines and circular town symbols in the style of old-fashioned cancellation marks
- Audio software with graphics simulating conventional stereo equipment
- The sound of a keyboard typing when using an automated phone system, as if a person is actually typing in your name or account number and looking you up in her records

These deliberate efforts to make customers more comfortable are brilliant in their simplicity. It's in our nature to resist new products because we tend to hold on to objects we're familiar with. Maintaining some resemblance to the product being replaced helps break down those barriers, giving us enough of a comfort level to invest a little effort in trying the newer version. When a manufacturer simulates a recognizable product attribute, we're more willing to accept the new product because the process or appearance looks or sounds familiar.

Using a skeuomorphic element is a clever, but sensible, way to show customers that you are in touch with their needs – that you are looking at the situation through their eyes. Designers and manufacturers must anticipate customer needs and reflect this with a strong attention to detail. Assume the role of trusted advisor, and customers will come to depend on you. When you help customers understand changes and improvements in terms of what is old and familiar, your organization is truly thinking like a customer.

The "WE" Approach

3D companies excel at creating improvements for customers even when customers aren't asking for them. That's when organizations really demonstrate that they are customer-centered. A captivating Mercedes-Benz commercial illustrates this with a tagline that says "Most people will never need ____, but we build it in anyway." The company inserts various features in the tagline, identifying aspects of their cars that differentiate them from competitors, but that also reflect an understanding of customer expectations of a high-end vehicle.

It's an example of the "WE" approach in action. "WE" – "What Else?" – reminds us to ask what else we can we do to make a process faster, simpler, or more intuitive for the customer. 3D businesses are always working to make life better for their customers. They talk with them to get their perspective and try to view products or services through customer eyes. They've learned that solving customer problems when they are still in the "opportunity" stage can help them develop close relationships with customers.

> The important thing is not to stop questioning.
> *Albert Einstein*

This results in the center of gravity shifting to the customer instead of the product. Thirty years ago, the customer didn't matter – it was a supplier's world. Today, the customer is the center of the business universe. Before, most of the information we needed was inside the company. Now it's on the outside, with the customer and the competition.

Companies answering the "what else?" question become adept at recognizing what's missing for the customer. As Marsha Brilliantes, senior accounting manager from cSubs believes, "The customer comes first. There is always an exception to the rule when taking care of customers. We figure out what the customer needs and treat every situation on a case-by-case basis."

Sometimes what's missing is an experience that's better than

103

ordinary. A company providing ordinary customer service might ask the question, "How did we deliver the product or the service based on our internal criteria?" while a 3D operation will ask, "What's the customer's reaction?" This evaluation goes far beyond correcting a problem or shortfall at the 1D transactional level. In 3D organizations, 1D performance should already be satisfactory. 3D providers are looking for ways to make ordinary service more remarkable.

Scott North of Barlean's tells his employees, "We want to be their favorite call of the week." Their approach is to always try to be more relatable to consumers. "Our people feel it when they are not hitting the mark," says North. "We also come up with ideas that we discuss within our department, such as 'wouldn't it be great if…' or 'how would they feel about….' "

What "Thinking Like a Customer" Means

> It is not an individual act, architecture. You have to consider your client. Only out of that can you produce great architecture. You cannot work in the abstract.
> *I.M. Pei*

As Barlean's illustrates, thinking like a customer is predicated on a vibrant, flexible 3D culture. This culture empowers each person in the business to become a solutions finder for customers. To optimize the company's 3D capability, each employee must understand and embrace the concept of the abundance gap.

Amazon.com continues to be a successful, strong brand because it always answers its business questions – strategic and day-to-day – with a solution that includes the customer. Jeff Bezos, Amazon's CEO, describes himself as "congenitally customer-focused." In its processes and culture, his company earns that customer-friendly status over and over, thanks to his leadership and strong sense of abundance. Bezos tells a story about billionaire Warren Buffett in which Buffett has three boxes on his desk: In-box, Out-box and Too-hard box. Bezos says that whenever his company is faced with one of those too-hard problems, employees ask, "Well, what's better for the customer?"

104   What a great message. The answers become much simpler when

we think like our customers. Ambiguity disappears because this approach clears the minds of employees and lets them focus on what the customer will value.

In order to grow, we need to constantly question what we are doing and how we can improve today's systems. We need to remember that the answers to our business questions should be customer-centered. In fact, that might be the only option in this fast-changing world. Organizational performance will be exponentially stronger if all employees feel they are doing everything they can for the customer.

That's the case at Barlean's, where employees asked the company to begin producing what became Forti-Flax, a ground flaxseed product. They knew it would help consumers. When talking with retailers about getting shelf placement, they were able to display it not only in the usual location, but also near the bananas, because it could be sprinkled on a banana for extra fiber. Placement near the banana section of the store also allows the retailer to offer samples.

Barlean's North adds, "We realized that we needed to make our products more prominent to retail customers in order to make them aware of their benefits. Instead of fighting the traditional challenges for shelf space, we developed a point of purchase display the retailer could place anywhere on the floor. It helped them – and it helped us."

Embracing this organizational philosophy creates a powerful foundation for designing dynamic corporate strategies, internal systems, and processes for getting work done in the ways that are most valuable to customer. The capability for thinking like a customer allows organizations to create in the "real world" rather than in isolation. At Barlean's, it equates to responsiveness, freedom and good health. It also means increasing service innovation at that company while creating an environment where people can be themselves. Barlean's managers always ask, "What's the outcome?", knowing that there are many ways to achieve it.

There's a gorgeous stand of rocks in the Grand Canyon that lets visitors see both east and west in the canyon. It's called "Ooh-Aah Point" because the view from the spot is simply amazing. Our work for customers should create the same feeling – "ooh-aah" instead of "ho-hum." When we are customers receiving great ideas from our suppliers, those ideas captivate us and pierce our natural defenses. We can't help but enjoy the experience. We should give our customers that positive experience, too.

Successful companies excel at ferreting out ho-hum customer experiences and figuring out ways to turn them into ooh-aah opportunities. They embed this thinking into their culture. They create new services by using a combination of deductive, inductive and abductive reasoning to imagine how a process could be better for customers. Just innovation, you say? Yes, but it is inevitably more effective and goal-driven when it is focused on making the experience more engaging and valuable to the customer.

Yesterday's practices are becoming inadequate as knowledgeable customers bring higher and higher expectations to their relationships with suppliers. When customer-centered organizations work to improve the customer experience, they inspire confidence in both customers and employees. What's missing in product-centric organizations is a system to design and deliver creative ideas that will improve the customer experience.

3D is Expansive

Picture the "pinch to expand" gesture that Apple has built into its iPhone and iPad devices. Customer 3D system expands an organization's performance in the same way that users expand graphics on these platforms. The customer doesn't stand still. Companies must reinvent products, processes and services to stay relevant and profitable. Always give more than you expect to receive. The secret is to give unselfishly. If you do it well, you will be rewarded later.

The Customer 3D system re-shapes the thinking of the organization. When we evaluate every decision and new idea based on the impact they will have on our customers, we're implementing a powerful manifesto for business growth. In contrast with a narrow 1D mindset directed at thinking only about your own organization, using 3D customer-centricity will take your business performance to the next dimension by building on abundance and active learning. Thinking like a customer provides the reach and depth that 1D organizations

106

do not have. It relies on anticipating an imagined future as if it were a present reality. Making these ideas happen, of course, requires work. But the power in the idea comes from treating a future event as if it has already happened, then setting about to take all of the necessary steps to make sure it does.

FIVE

Customer Strategy

*The essence of strategy is in choosing to
perform activities differently or
to perform different activities than rivals.*
Michael Porter

Businesses traditionally have a product strategy detailing how products should be positioned in the market and a financial strategy outlining how they'll reach revenue goals. Most, however, don't have a customer strategy that defines how the organization will behave for or toward customers. What a shame – and what a loss for them.

3D companies create customer strategies because they know that pushing products onto markets isn't nearly as effective as pulling customers in to create a closeness that leads to long-lasting and mutually productive relationships. A 3D customer strategy involves doing the right thing to help customers accomplish better outcomes, whether those outcomes are improved health, becoming more efficient, or being able to do things more quickly. With this type of strategy, employees are empowered to always be mindful of what's best for the customer. In that sense, it's an employee strategy, too.

This is an important chapter in the journey to becoming a truly 3D organization because it establishes the ground rules for how this new customer-centered culture will behave and what the destination will look like. It won't happen without a customer strategy.

Re-Orienting the Organization

The caution sign in Figure 5.1 illustrates what must happen in organizations working to meet customer needs. Companies know their direction – the lower vertical line heading upward – but are stuck when they hit a roadblock, which might be a need for new ideas. The solution is to shift – illustrated by the horizontal line – to a customer-centered approach. By thinking expansively about "unmet customer needs," any business can take off with a fresh, invigorated energy that will lead to a much higher performance and rise to the top, in the direction of that caution sign arrow.

Figure 5.1

Many organizations are bothered that they can't make change happen by simply tweaking their existing system. But tomorrow's success doesn't come from yesterday's thinking. Barb Bloch of Barlean's says that "We are now developing a new product for the pet industry which will help animals with health issues. I suggested this to management and the company has been supportive of my ideas and wants to provide a product which will make pets healthier." Dramatic change can only happen through commitment to a heuristic system that enables organizations to focus on designing products and services driven by customer needs. That's how breakthrough thinking takes off.

Think of it as a re-mastering process. Just as technology can make a new master tape from an old one in a way that improves the fidelity of the original recording, embracing a Customer 3D philosophy can help re-master our organizations, too. This is important because we can no longer expect to find and retain customers through wishful thinking. We need a well-thought-out 3D customer strategy.

The customer strategy of a 3D company establishes parameters on the low end and stretch goals on the high end for acceptable employee behaviors. In contrast, 1D organizations lack a focused customer strategy. They are limited, at best, to a vague "take care of the customer" mantra. These one-dimensional, product-centric organizations tend to set financial and operational strategies only, hoping the customer will be willing to work with them on the company's terms. This usually means following the vendor's policies and procedures.

As the design of the new Customer 3D strategy evolves, it creates an organization that customers understand and love. A customer strategy in a 3D organization will:

- Be organization-wide, not hit-and-miss, or territorial
- Have equal importance to its product strategy and its financial strategy to balance decision-making
- Be specific about what the organization does and doesn't do to bring value to its customers
- Define positive outcomes, with goals, that will impact customers
- Protect customers, almost as a parent would protect a child, by empowering employees to work in the best interest of customers

A Customer-Centered Strategy

What would happen if you developed a specific strategy designed to focus your organization on becoming more customer-centered? It would take your company to a new dimension, one that would transform your performance in the eyes of customers, wouldn't it? Who wouldn't want that? The boundaries that separate you from your customers would begin to disappear, replaced instead by steady growth. It would take your organization to a new dimension, one where your customers believe you're outperforming your competitors.

> A strategy is not a goal or an objective or a target. It's not a vision or mission or a statement of purpose. It's about being different from rivals in some important way.
> *Phil Rosenzweig*

Most companies acknowledge that their strategy is to make profits or maximize return to their shareholders. This isn't bad, of course, but it's difficult to engage employees in this strategy because, from their perspective, their job is to manage the organization's relationship with its customers. They leave that whole "management of profits" mystery to the executive suite. A customer strategy can do wonders

III

to align the organization around a common goal that's relevant to all.

Picture a mound of 10,000 iron shavings, each one representing an employee in a business. Each shaving points in a different direction because, well, that's what iron shavings do. Now imagine that each one of those iron shavings represents an employee. They could all be smart people working very hard to make what they think are the right decisions, but the net result is confusion. As David Collis and Michael Rukstad note in "Can You Say What Your Strategy Is?" in the *Harvard Business Review*, "If you pass a magnet over those filings, what happens? They line up."[1] A customer-centered business strategy acts like that magnet. It aligns those iron shavings – employees – in the same direction because they're focused on outperforming for your customers. When that happens, anything is possible. It's a philosophy rather than a technique or method. It expands the development of your company's capacities for new ideas while it stimulates constructive change in everyone.

The end result is a growth-promoting climate throughout your organization because it focuses the entire system on how it can do things differently or better for customers. As Collis and Rukstad point out, "Clarity about what makes the firm distinctive is what most helps employees understand how they can contribute."[2]

A clear change in your strategy will have a significant impact that makes a big difference in your performance. Balance your strategy around delivering innovative ideas and services that your competitors aren't offering, then watch employees act with greater confidence because they will understand their roles much more clearly. And the profits will come.

Customer Barriers

A barrier between customers and employees gets in the way of creating a customer strategy. Many companies say they don't have barriers between them and their customers, but is that really true? These boundaries have been standard operating procedure for decades because companies have focused their strategies on products and services, not on the customer. What was called the "customer experience" was simply a description of how these products were delivered. Today, organizations are more mindful of customer connections that are deeper and solutions-focused.

Every company needs a customer strategy that is clear and succinct, one that employees can internalize. They need a guide they can use when making difficult decisions. Take these steps when creating a strategy that will guide employees:

- Define what the strategy should achieve for the customer. How will the customer benefit?
- Eliminate fragmentation or internal silos that will be visible to the customer.
- Simplify what you are doing based on what the customer sees, not on what is efficient for you.
- Educate your customers as much as possible.
- Deliver new ideas, products, or processes, even if the customer hasn't asked for them.
- Offer new ideas, products, or processes that will make the customer more successful.

A customer strategy needs to be descriptive, but not rigid. It can't be too broad, expecting employees to be everything to everyone. It should, though, be proactive and focused rather than reactive, where the company waits for the customer to ask for something before responding. A 3D customer strategy must articulate a basic philosophy that aligns all employees, bringing confidence and clarity to their efforts to generate stronger customer connections. It's worth noting that it shouldn't be necessary to address courtesy, hospitality and helpfulness, since those attributes should already be part of the organization's culture.

The process of defining a customer strategy involves focusing on the customer in a way that balances with strategies for finance and product performance.

Elements of a 3D Customer Strategy

3D leaders align employees around a strategy that is focused on the customer and uses products or services the organization sells to help customers. Customer-centricity "completes" the organization – it's not seen as something that interferes with the company's purpose. Customer 3D organizations design their customer strategy to challenge the organization to do three things very well:

113

1. **They generate ideas that add value.** New, customer-centric ideas are required for a company's customer strategy. These come through observation of customer needs, which leads to proactive ideas about ways to do things better, faster, or more simply. 3D cultures empower their employees to continually ask, "What else does the customer need from our systems?"

2. **They are aggressive silo-busters.** 3D companies succeed in part because they require permeable "walls" between functional areas. This permeability creates strong communication, which allows process improvements to happen seamlessly. 3D performers are excellent at simplifying processes by questioning any unnecessary complexity that customers experience.

3. **They're good storytellers.** Every 3D business uses the art of storytelling to praise great performances by individual employees who have helped customers. This praise, in turn, encourages similar behaviors throughout the organization.

3D organizations are future-oriented. They articulate a clear strategy for making their customers better by empowering employees to operate well above the break-even point in Figure 4.1. Going well beyond customer satisfaction, they create a giving, human culture throughout the organization, which instills an energy that focuses on customers. It will help to learn more about each trait here.

Trait 1: Ideas That Add Value

One of the best ways to add value is to simplify processes. This requires observation, thought, creativity, and effort, but it is well worth it. Why? Because when customers view your processes as overly complex, they get the impression that you are unresponsive – and this makes them more vulnerable to competitor poaching. If we focus on simplifying things in ways that customers notice, we end up with a business that is clear, pragmatic and intuitive. Anybody can understand a straightforward outcome, not just the creators. Customer-centric companies make the ability to keep products and services simple a core value.

The Strong's success with museum-going customers has, in part, developed out of a focus on keeping it simple. As Kathie Dengler, senior vice president for guest and institutional services explains it, "There are complicated situations, but they don't take complicated solutions." For example, one guest was using the old "Dad said it was okay with him if it was okay with you" technique to bring her child into the museum without paying by approaching a different host each time, claiming that another host had said the child didn't need to pay. When the hosts talked to each other later, they realized that this had happened too many times. The next time the woman tried this method, a host directed her outside of the child's hearing range to explain that they would admit both her and the child that day so that the child wasn't disappointed, but that they wouldn't give the child free admission again. He was, essentially, saying, "We're on to you, but we don't want to hurt your child." The conversation was simple and direct.

Emphasizing simplification does two things. First, it forces us to ask, "What is really necessary?" We're compelled to peel away complexity to find a process that is clear and near-perfect for the customer. We might still be able to improve it, but it's closer to the way it should be. An employee of one of our manufacturing clients figured this out on his own and simplified things for a customer by designing a one-piece part to replace the existing two-piece version. Was the customer pleased? You bet. The new part was easier to use and saved the customer money, too.

Secondly, simplification unites your culture with a common goal: To keep it simple. Customers really do appreciate simple, especially when it seems like the obvious choice. Look in your own life for examples. Most of us need to reset digital clocks when the U.S. switches from daylight saving time (DST) to standard time or when the power goes out. On most devices, it's bothersome to change the hour, especially if the clock is designed so that we have to click forward ahead 23 hours to set the time back one hour. It's not something that we complain to the manufacturer about, though, and it's not a feature we look for on the packaging when we purchase a clock. And yet, even though we don't complain, the designers of the iHome® radio added a button to the back of the appliance that toggles between a -1/+1 DST setting. With one click, the clock resets the hour without changing the reading for the minutes. I appreciate the classic simplicity of the process. It humanizes the technology.

> Good ideas are built out of a collection of existing parts.
> *Steven Johnson*

Mechanistic 1D businesses believe that complicated is better than simple. With this 1D thinking comes the tendency to hang around waiting for that one big breakthrough idea. 3D organizations add value to customers by pursuing incremental improvements instead. Steven Johnson refers to these opportunities as the "adjacent possible."[3] They build on existing concepts and practices. Customer 3D develops these positive changes by framing them in the context of customer needs and then aggressively working out the solution. Innovation isn't just a journey, it's a workout.

Subscription management company cSubs provides an example of how this works. One of its customers said her company is continually impressed with the new ideas cSubs offers. "They have quarterly meetings with us, sharing new ideas for how we can save money," she explains. "And they will customize systems to deliver outcomes that we didn't have before." Imagine how it would feel if your clients talked about your company this way!

We aren't successful if we don't add value somehow to customers. A mandate to simplify encourages employees to focus on helping customers accomplish a task in fewer steps. It's not possible, though, unless the outcome is clearly defined. The Customer 3D system provides that definition. It motivates employees to explore new ideas, gives them other ideas for context, and shows them where this effort fits in with the entire organization. In addition, it provides a setting for these employees to test their ideas and to learn from the testing.

Anti-Complexity Officer

You can always become a hero with customers by keeping it simple. We have enough complexity already. Because of that, we have less and less patience with suppliers that expect us to figure out how to do business with them.

> Simplicity is the ultimate sophistication.
> *Leonardo da Vinci*

We've have heard a lot in recent years about the chief customer officer. I'd like to see customer strategies include an anti-complexity officer (ACO) who advocates for simplified processes for customers. Job duties might include making certain there are never any internal compromises when the customer is involved, or helping the organization develop a system for finding and eliminating customer process complexity.

Business success certainly depends on adding value for customers, but it requires reducing headaches for these customers, too. Make your anti-complexity officer responsible for finding and eliminating nuisance factors and steps that are illogical or even boring to customers. The ACO can create process simplifications that the customer will notice and appreciate.

The classic *Harvard Business Review* article, "Staple Yourself to an Order,"[4] challenged us to manage the 20th Century order cycle process to reduce problems for customers. Fewer problems, of course, would result in better customer satisfaction. In the 21st Century, however, the "staple-yourself" concept has taken on new meaning. Years ago, while the approach might have reduced order errors, the process was still built for the seller's efficiency. Customer-centric organizations are now re-designing these processes with the customer in mind – and they're seeing greater customer loyalty as well as brand positioning as the company that cares about the customer.

As Warren Buffett's mentor, Benjamin Graham, observed, "In the short term, the market is a voting machine. In the long term, it is a weighing machine."[5] The ACO will help build internal processes that optimize delivery of complete solutions to customers, which, in turn, will make life easier for these customers. The ACO will focus the company on "what works for the customer" rather than what is efficient internally. This optimization will inevitably favor the long-term "weight" that the market will assign to your company.

Every touch point that is confusing will eventually lead to customer defection. As a C-level executive, the ACO will own the processes that once grew out of convenience for the company and become inconveniences for customers – or, even worse, as unnecessarily frustrating for them. An ACO can help create an organization that is focused on thinking like its customers – one that customers will understand.

Trait 2: Silo-busting Permeability
The Customer 3D system helps companies dissolve the separation

between departments and the territorial mentality that is often referred to as silos. At engineering and contracting firm MESA, for example, John Cole, VP of Sales and Business Development, talks about how MESA's departments collaborate routinely in ways that benefit both MESA and its customer. "I received an e-mail from our South Carolina office regarding work for a large client that needed specific testing done. Our competitor had promised them the world, but the material was not working. To help out, we organized special training for our sales people, got the information we needed because it was a specialized custom project, and had the operations group tackle it," he says.

The job was completed in a short period of time because MESA understood the requirements and could move from engineering to manufacturing to installation quickly. "I can't tell you how impressed the customer was," Cole says, adding that the company has since become a regular customer. This experience is routine for 3D organizations.

In 3D organizations, everyone "owns" the company's relationship with its customers. MESA's commitment to that philosophy shows in its telephone support. "Many customers tell us that they appreciate getting a 'live' person when they call us because they love the human touch. It reinforces that we go above and beyond for our customers," Sarfraz says.

At cSubs, the same alignment drives customer-centricity. "We see ideas and try to group them differently to make processes more streamlined," says MacKenzie Shirm, customer support representative. "For example, by working together, we recently changed how we handle the way clients order corporate licenses. Clients can do it themselves online or they can contact us – whichever approach is easier."

"We are all very flexible when it comes to helping each other," adds Marsha Brilliantes, senior accounting manager. "Our teamwork is all geared toward our customers. When there's a large special client project, the staff will not hesitate to ask for help, because people will all chip in."

118   What happens when different areas of the company have different

views of customer needs? For example, what should happen if Engineering wants to design a highly effective product which they believe the customer will want and Marketing believes that the customer will not like it and will not buy it? The solution, of course, is to experiment and find out what the customer prefers. Use prototypes with target consumers.

Models make it easier to change your mind. It shows the potential of any idea. It turns the reality of the moment into a better, more desirable reality for the customer. How intense is the emotional reaction? That intensity will drive customers' behavior. Ideas happen best when they develop out of collaboration – when they are seen as necessary, rather than mandated by one portion of the company.

Trait 3: Storytelling and Praise

In 3D organizations, the customer-centric culture keeps expanding because of the positive communication from the leaders about doing the right thing. They praise employees who do things that add value to customers, sharing their stories with others. These stories motivate employees to believe in themselves and the entire organization. This is why it's important for management to reinforce the behaviors that support the company's culture.

> **Celebrate what you want to see more of.**
> *Tom Peters*

At financial advisory firm Veritat Advisors, shared stories help employees stay excited about the way the company helps customers. For example, advisors called one couple to warn them that their account balance was dangerously low. The clients were surprised because they hadn't been paying close enough attention, but they were equally grateful that the firm alerted them. Sharing this story with employees helps them visualize the type of honest, responsible advice the firm wants to be known for.

Customer 3D organizations know how to reinforce strong cultures by spreading the word through success stories. That's why the 3D organizations featured in this book have been willing to share information here – they know the value of explaining what they've done for customers and how those customers have reacted. Their stories illustrate how their culture consistently walks the talk. "Stories are the currency of human growth," says Jean Houston, one

119

of the founders of the Human Potential Movement. In 3D companies, because employees understand their organization's purpose, they become active participants in creating and telling its story.

Stories reinforce good practices that might otherwise go unnoticed. At Barlean's Organic Oils, management shares stories at monthly employee lunch meetings by reading letters from customers explaining how Barlean's has changed their lives. People in all departments – even those without direct customer interaction – have an opportunity to learn from and appreciate these positive customer experiences.

cSubs reinforces the importance of storytelling at its all-company quarterly awards meetings, where they share the stories that generate the awards. At daily pre-shift meetings at The Strong museum, employees share stories about great service they've seen on the job recently.

3D organizations also educate with legacy storytelling because they all know that the values that made their companies successful in the early years are the ones that will enhance customer centeredness. The Microsoft Museum is a great example of storytelling about the history of the company, its products and its culture. In every company, this helps employees make the connection between the present and the past and it shapes the potential future.

The Strong has a culture that encourages storytelling among its employees as a way to continually improve customer services. Dengler says, "We also have circle time before every shift, with up to 30 hosts attending. We prepare them for the day by letting them hear what is going on in the museum that they should be aware of and debrief them if, for example, we expect a greater number of guests for a mid-term school break or another event. We sometimes do scavenger hunts to make them feel more familiar with the museum. We also ask them to share any stories that they can tell about great service that was delivered. We use storytelling a lot in our training. Our criterion for hosts is that they are mentor-ready to train other hosts."

120 For example, the empowerment culture at The Strong encourages

hosts to implement new ideas to help customers without asking permission. When a guest that had donated a large Transformer figure to the museum wanted to propose to his girlfriend in front of the display, employees at The Strong built a mount to set on the model that looked like the figure was actually holding the ring when the couple arrived.

It might seem at first that storytelling does little to improve the customer experience. However, it's the primary means of reinforcing the behaviors an organization values. It fuels the system by demonstrating the frequency of positive customer-centered activities and reinforces positive behaviors for everyone in the organization. Public praise across the company will support the creativity revealed by the stories. It will also extend these activities as the stories get re-told to co-workers and customers.

When storytelling becomes part of the culture, the organization sees a number of significant shifts in behavior and thinking, including:

- Employees start having fun as they enjoy more freedom and a sense of empowerment
- Employees take pride in the work their company is doing
- Customer outcomes, not competitor product or service differences, become the key differentiators
- The focus shifts to the organization's ability to help customers make money in their businesses
- When employees hear positive stories, they stop keeping to themselves and become empowered to create more stories

3D progress becomes steady and meaningful when the vision is constantly repeated; stories help do that.

Praise is Inherent in the Storytelling Process.

"Praise is a very important part of our culture," says Kathie Dengler of The Strong. "We praise employees publicly and individually. This is more effective than general praise when it isn't due." Dengler also reviews and follows up on all comment cards. If there's a positive comment with no employee name linked to it, she researches the date, time and place in the museum to identify the individual, then sends an "I am grateful" note. Not only does this praise make the employee proud, but it models the type of behavior the museum wants for all employees. It lets people see the impact they have on guests.

Barlean's won the best new product at a recent industry trade show. Following is the message that CIO Jade Beutler sent to the entire company:

> *YOU have done it AGAIN!*
>
> *Hello, fellow Barlean's Team Elite!*
>
> *Just when you thought things could not get any better at Barlean's we are ONCE AGAIN honored with an incredible distinction and award.*
>
> *BEST NEW PRODUCT OF NATURAL PRODUCTS EXPO WEST!!!!*
>
> *To appreciate the full gravity of this honor you need to consider the enormity of the Expo West show. The trade show floor stretches for city blocks – with thousands of companies exhibiting and probably a million products represented. SO – that means that Barlean's Blackberry Swirl is a ONE IN A MILLION product!*
>
> *Please consider your role in the creation and or support of this amazing product. EVERYONE in the company has touched this product and contributed to its success in some way! SWIRL is one in a million because YOU are one in a million.*
>
> *I am absolutely humbled by the recognition that we have received and hope never to take your excellence nor the excellence of our products and success for granted. Please just take a moment in reflection and appreciation for what you have done as it is truly exceptional. JOB WELL DONE!*
>
> *On behalf of the Barlean's family – Thank You! Jade*

David Rifkin, executive vice-president at cSubs, explains the format of their company meetings: "First we welcome everyone and discuss company news, about clients or systems improvements. Then we announce the employee incentive points that have been earned. With these points, we believe in sharing the story of what was specifically done and we always ask the employee to tell the story from his or her point of view. Employees always know good things will happen in these meetings."

Customer-Friendly Speed Bumps

A customer strategy needs to be evaluated according to how customers will react. If rules and procedures are too cumbersome, a 3D organization takes steps to make them more practical from the customer's viewpoint. Every organization creates default procedures that guide customer decisions and behaviors. These defaults can be helpful and expedient or restrictive and exploitative. Companies that use them, however, should decide whether the decision tree of choices offered to customers are product-centric or customer-centric.

Default procedures essentially manage customer behavior by limiting choices. Sometimes, these constraints can be positive. A chime in your car reminding you to fasten your seat belt encourages safe habits. An online product purchase form that defaults to less expensive "standard shipping" is convenient and probably serves the needs of the majority. But some defaults can frustrate or even alienate customers – do yours? When there are too many options, decision-making can come to a standstill. We need to be careful to give choices – but not so many choices that our customer becomes paralyzed.

Think of a restrictive default procedure as a speed bump. To make sure we drive sensibly in certain areas, builders install speed bumps that force us to slow down. From my perspective, they're the epitome of frustration because they aren't adaptable to users. That could change, though, because Mexico-based Decano Industries is developing a device that automatically retreats back into the ground when we're driving the speed limit or slower. When the sensor knows that we're driving too fast, the bump stays up. It's a proactive, customer-friendly innovation that rewards acceptable behavior and attempts to change what's unacceptable. It's a default with options.

There's a trend toward more personalized or "smart" defaults, such as always providing a non-smoking hotel room unless a smoking room is requested, or automatically adapting next steps in online

123

environments according to answers to previous questions. For example, an auto manufacturer using an online "select your features" shopping function can recommend a sportier steering wheel style when the shopper has already selected a high-horsepower engine during an automobile configuration. The ability to think like a customer is essential to perfecting a customer default procedure. When the end result is more customer-centered, it's worth it. What matters most is the logic and authenticity of the customer experience.

Customer relationships with suppliers or vendors will be exponentially stronger if customers believe that organizations understand them and have provided a streamlined experience based on that understanding. Organizations that design customer-centered default procedures will be rewarded with loyalty and trust.

Staying Ahead

All organizational change, whether it comes from the ACO's efforts or anywhere else, should have an impact on the customer. Why change if the customer doesn't notice it? There's no point in changing if it doesn't add value to the customer. Unfortunately for them, one-dimensional companies don't want to accept this – they'd rather avoid the concept and hold tightly to their products and procedures instead. 1D businesses prefer operating in the traditional world in which they use Six Sigma programs or lean initiatives to make internal changes which, they believe, aren't noticeable to customers.

Customer 3D, on the other hand, allows organizations to stay ahead of customer change. It's thrilling for a business to be so proactive that it's ahead of the curve rather than chasing to catch up with its customers. We aren't talking about party tricks or superficial techniques, either – we're talking about a different way of thinking. It's architecture, not bricklaying. It requires clarity of vision and a compelling message for both customers and employees.

The most important question that every organization must answer is, "How can we continue to improve for the customer?" 3D organizations are always working on that; their strategy is to never stand still on the path to becoming more customer-centered and 3D.

124   Because of online retailer Amazon's fast-changing markets, founder

Jeff Bezos believes that it helps to base your strategy on things that won't change. He asks his senior team, "What's not going to change in the next five years?" Invariably, the answers always revolve around customer insights. For example, they understand that customers will continue to want lower prices, so they must always be working on reducing problems with orders and improving efficiency. Customers will also want greater convenience and more transparency, so suppliers can't be satisfied with the status quo. In a world in which the change is happening more quickly than ever and people are taking wrong turns with their businesses, customers are the constant that can keep our decisions grounded.

Amazon has a powerful mission to support the concept of customer-centricity, not just within the company, but "across the entire business world." Bezos wants to "be stubborn of the vision; be flexible of the details." Like every 3D organization, Amazon's leaders answer all internal questions with the customer in mind. The danger with product-centered companies is that their products cause them to become so self-absorbed that they ignore what customers want or need. This leads to distrust among customers. Product-centric changes often amount to technology solutions looking for a problem, but the opposite should be your organization's model. Customer 3D helps organizations shake up the way they think, something that's necessary in a competitive environment. And if change doesn't help the customer, it will cause discomfort.

The customer doesn't stand still – he isn't even the same as he was even one or two years ago. Needs change. Expectations change. Situations change. Yet, most organizations don't recognize, realize, or accept this. Their heads are stuck in the sand, so to speak, where it's easier to believe that products and services they provided two years ago will continue to make the business successful. And while it's true that we can't predict the future, I'm pretty certain that if what you're doing now is the same as what you did a year ago, your future will include dissatisfied customers who are thinking about leaving you.

A Strategy of Adding Value
Because 1D organizations are blinded by their traditional way of doing business, they lose sight of their customers' key priorities. They tend to rely on information provided by market research that

125

is too removed from the customer, tries to measure too much and is therefore too general or vague, and asks the wrong questions. A situation like this – when the 1D organization is operating almost blindly – presents newcomers with plenty of opportunities for assessing which customer priorities are being ignored by incumbent suppliers – then stepping in to fill the gap.

Future-oriented organizations are changing this approach in ways that resemble highly effective detective work. Findings must be fact-based and customer-connected. Otherwise, these companies will never significantly improve the value they provide. Strategic, customer-centric thinking uses insights from well-designed research to proactively identify changes in customer priorities. Knowing and understanding how customer priorities are changing is essential and powerful.

The irony is that you have the ability to connect with and understand your customers better than any of your competitors, but you often don't recognize it. In *The Profit Zone*, Adrian J. Slywotzky and David Morrison explain it this way: "Incumbent companies have the advantage of easy access to the customer, but it is their most underutilized asset."[6]

Correct – because you're the incumbent, you have the best access to your customers, and yet, you operate in your own product-centric world, dealing with the issues that matter to you, not your customers.

Actively research and listen to your customers so you can define what is important to them going forward – not just how you are performing right now. Find out which of their priorities are being ignored. Then attack those unfulfilled priorities with a vengeance. Create the solutions that your customers want, and you will lock in your status at the same time. Design your business to be the one that best addresses and serves the customer's most important priorities.

Transformer insulation manufacturer WEIDMANN Electrical Technology, Inc. excels in listening to customers. Its Joint Engineering Cost Reduction Team meets every six months to evaluate opportunities to assist at the facilities of its insulation design customers. Team members do walk-throughs at the plants to identify ways to save money and increase productivity. In addition, its engineering team's regular one-on-one interviews with customers help the engineers fully understand customer needs, or to help them uncover production bottlenecks. They share all of the ideas that come from these on-site visits in an idea bank that's accessible to everyone else at WEIDMANN, too, so employees can learn from the experiences of colleagues.

Success today is predicated on designing your business around what you have learned from customers. Organizations that want to outperform are developing internal cultures that are learning how to think like a customer – as WEIDMANN does. Companies must reinvent to stay relevant and solve customer problems in order to move into new profit areas.

All of us know that change is omnipresent and that we must react to it. The Customer 3D system transforms organizations that want to become more customer-centric. It takes them from a place where they're thinking about product competency to one where they're expanding to understand how their actions will impact their relevance to customers. The organizations that can use customer closeness to stay ahead of the changing priorities of those same customers will be the innovators who own the future.

3D

Google Sketch Up. Google's 3D software, Sketch Up, includes a Follow Me Tool which allows the designer to extrude one shape into a 3D version that solves specific design problems, without having to re-draw the shape to meet specific requirements. The molding on a building, for example, is a flat shape that has been extruded to transition or bridge two surfaces.

How can your organization reinforce its customer-centered strategy by extruding a 3D performance in one area of the organization across the entire culture?

Figure 5.2 *Image courtesy of www.sketchup.google.com*

What Can Your Customers Accomplish?

There's a difference between providing your customers with the product or service they expect and helping them achieve what they care about, though. How would it feel to offer your customers something that didn't cost you anything, but gave them a powerful sense of accomplishment? That is part of the strategy of 3D organizations.

CP Rochester, a Rochester, N.Y., nonprofit that helps children and adults with disabilities, knows how to do this. Sara Dankert, one of its employees, became an advocate for Jane, a client, several years ago. She helped Jane develop her interest in art. Through the years, Jane created a number of paintings that Sara helped her exhibit. Another client, Jeff, eventually joined Jane in her art show and they sold their work to raise money for the nonprofit. Ironically, their art, once a vehicle for expressing themselves, became a way to support others that they cared about. It doesn't get much better than that.

This story goes far beyond helping these two art lovers, though. It's rewarding on three levels. First, Jane not only felt greater self-esteem, she also enjoyed a sense of accomplishment. In the recent book *Spiral Up*, author Jane Linder[7] says that the emotional hooks that energize people include winning, striving, belonging, creating, independence, and contributing or giving. Artist Jane felt all of these emotions when she made a difference for others.

At another level, however, Dankert felt rewarded because she had facilitated a process that helped her client – her customer – develop. This process wouldn't have happened without her. This epitomizes the "thinking like a customer" approach. Dankert went far beyond the expected performance to help her client find and enjoy abundance. Both benefit from the ongoing initiatives. "We both needed the project to motivate us and to show each other what we are capable of doing," Dankert says. It starts with connections between people, but, she adds, "We push each other to go further and do greater things."

At a third level, this mutually beneficial relationship served as an amazing example of what's possible for Dankert colleagues at the agency. She modeled impressive behavior, paving the way for others in the nonprofit to take their own creative ideas to the next level to help customers express themselves.

All organizations become more successful when they think in terms of helping their customers achieve more. Instead of simply serving customers, high-performing organizations empathize with them. When we understand what customers are passionate about and are capable of accomplishing, we simply need to give them a boost. When we embrace this as our jobs, our work becomes transformational for both us and our customers.

Customers want a sense of accomplishment, but we don't often give them that opportunity. Give them goals they really care about. Provide a direction and a start, then let them complete the task. The payback is just as satisfying for you and your organization. The impact of the art created by Jane and Jeff made as much of an impact on Dankert, their mentor, as it did for the artists themselves.

How many companies do you know that have reached out to customers to help them accomplish something they never thought possible? If you empower your customers, they will always remember you.

Balanced Business Goals

A strong customer strategy will provide balance with the product and financial strategies that are already in place. We're reading more and more lately about right-brain thinking – finally. Business has traditionally been left-brained, but its ability to search for greater efficiencies and to innovate while lowering costs has reached a plateau. The new opportunity to take performance to the next level comes through right-brain thinking. It's a shift that recognizes how our customers want us to interact with them.

Right-brainers reason holistically, recognize patterns and interpret emotions. Right-brain people tend to approach every business situation from the customer's point of view. Right brain thinking is considered creative and intuitive while left brain thinking is analytical and sequential. Here's how right brain and left brain thinking breaks down[8]:

129

Right brain thinking:	Left brain thinking:
Interprets things simultaneously	Interprets in sequences
Specializes in context	Sees text
Synthesizes the big picture	Analyzes details
Focuses on relationships	Focuses on categories

Customer-centered thinking puts us in a position to notice things we hadn't noticed before. The more vigorous the re-orientation in this direction, the greater the potential for innovation and breakthroughs in our business. It puts demands on our imagination, enlarging our approach to decision-making in a way that sets it free. In terms of thinking like a customer, the creative "right" side of our brains can also serve as a lie detector for products and services created in an analog world.

There's a whole new business performance category in which both sides must work together. Right-brain thinking is essential to catalyzing our services and tempering the narrow, flat 1D, left-brain solutions. Customer-centric organizations are right-brained and expansive. 3D organizations leverage this underutilized perspective to set proactive business goals that will jump-start business growth.

Right brain thought is a specialty skill (just as left-brain thought is) that should force our organizations to challenge each decision with the "How it will affect the customer?" test. The most distinctive feature of a customer-centric business is the way it implicitly anticipates and responds to changes that are valued by customers. Sure, there will be tension between the right- and left-brain approaches to serving customers, but that tension shouldn't get in the way of the organization's performance. It should, instead, be one of its prime resources. It should balance our strategy as both sides work together.

3D culture building creates a balanced strategy that is centered on delivering extraordinary results for customers. This culture begins and continues because of positive leaders who understand that thinking like a customer generates energy that expands the organization beyond one-dimensional flatness. Customers, then, are viewed as the source of much higher performance – if we pay attention to them. We will perform better for them when we fully understand them.

The Customer's Customer

Truly customer-centered organizations have a strategy for all of their customers – even the customers who don't buy directly from them.

Most organizations have customers they sell to directly – primary customers. Those, in turn, might assemble, distribute, enhance or otherwise add value to their purchase so they can sell it to other customers – they're the first company's secondary customers. Today, many companies say they're selling solutions, rather than products, because products can be turned into commodities too easily. They don't realize that they will do a much better job of selling when they approach the sale to the primary customer with a strong understanding of the unmet needs of the secondary customer.

Customer-centered businesses, whether business-to-business or business-to-consumer, are consistently working to understand the primary customer's end application and approaching the current challenges of the secondary customer as if they were their own. "Solution selling" must go beyond learning about what the customer asks for. It must anticipate secondary customer needs and find ways to solve their problems more intuitively. It must be proactive and look for opportunities that the primary customer might not even see. The best way to add value is to help those primary customers have a better outcome that they can sell, in turn, to their customers.

Graham Milner of WD-40, for example, feels strongly that "the end-user must be involved in describing the white space (i.e., the areas in which their needs are not being met)." Then, his team uses that information to improve the product or process to take care of those needs more effectively.

Suppliers are more capable of finding solutions when they anticipate future needs. This culture shift is stronger than simply listening to customers. Learning will translate into the entire organization improving in the eyes of the customer. It qualifies all employees to do their present tasks with continually wider vision and continually increasing competence.

131

In what ways will the customer's technology progress in the next two to three years? Customer-centric suppliers want to help their primary customers succeed by creating new ideas for those secondary customers because this will give both organizations every advantage over the competition. Barlean's customer strategy is not to sell products, but instead to try to add more value. "We want to leave them with the feeling that they spent their time wisely," Terence Klein, social media administrator, observes. Although Barlean's can sell and ship directly to consumers, they forward those opportunities to retailers whenever possible. Innovation for secondary customers turns customer-centered suppliers into heroes in the eyes of their primary customers.

Suppliers are much more valuable to their direct customers when they help them meet their markets' unmet needs. Solution-selling must be customer-centered. To be successful, it must make the primary customer's product better in the eyes of the secondary customer. It has to be focused on the customer's customer.

3D Sound Bites

Every Customer 3D organization has a catch phrase that reinforces what they want to achieve with their customers. It sums up the customer attitude they want their employees to embrace, day in and day out. Here are a few that truly resonate:

- WD-40 Company: "We are in the memories business."
- Barlean's Organic Oils: "We want to be our customers' favorite call for the week."
- cSubs Corporate Subscription Management Services: "We treat our clients as family members."
- MESA Products: "It's personal. Building trust and being honest creates relationships with our customers."
- Microsoft: "Be What's Next" for our customers.
- WEIDMANN Electrical Technology, Inc.: "We speak the same language as our customers."
- The Strong: "People first. Things second."

These companies have used their customer strategies to create the slogans. For the employees, they act as a shorthand that represents the company's full customer strategy. The catchphrases are the rallying point.

No Mixed Messages

Sometimes, leaders deliver mixed messages regarding customer focus. They tell employees to take care of customers but expect the organization to remain product-centered, which can confuse employees. What results is a shallow 1D message that will ultimately hold back any real progress toward customer-centricity. In addition, 1D leaders don't always understand the work that's necessary to make the organization customer-centric. They wrongly assume that "getting closer to the customer" is easy.

Outperforming for your customers is about educating the entire company, starting with your executives, about two things: How to think like a customer, and how the process of becoming 3D happens within the organization. It is naïve to believe that anyone and everyone in your workforce can automatically think like a customer. It has to be taught, aggressively pursued as a "milestone," and monitored.

Thinking like a customer represents dramatic change. It involves looking at every detail from your customers' viewpoint. It also requires every employee's active input. It must be centered on a shared dream about how the future will be better. And it requires leadership that builds momentum by reminding everyone that the organization can always get better at thinking like a customer.

Start with a Single Touch Point

Becoming customer-centric requires a strategy for change in both a company's culture and its process design. It demands a long-term commitment that involves everyone in your organization. Still, we might be intimidated by the prospect if we view the customer-centric identity as a destination that we reach only after a long journey. It works better if we think of it instead as a workout. Just like exercise, the benefits only happen if we stay committed to the program, but we get healthier, stronger, and more fit every day.

The challenge is getting started, and getting started in a way that generates the results that keep us going. There is one proven method

133

to jump-start the process in a way that will accelerate the company-wide commitment to the journey: You start by improving one specific customer touch point. And you get the leaders involved in the process, too, so that they're experiencing the process alongside the employees who are the most passionate and customer-centric already.

Every touch point with customers represents an opportunity. Each employee becomes an advocate for the customer inside the organization – a different take on the 'voice of the customer' phrase – infusing the customer into every decision-making system inside the company. They use heightened observation techniques to guide them to inspiration and comprehension. It creates a homogeneous culture because working for the customer is seen as everyone's business. It provides a context for conversations about the customer. It unifies employees around a common purpose.

Re-constructing a 3D customer-centered corporate identity creates a spirit focused on finding new answers and overcoming constraints. It's the gestalt of the organization, as perceived by customers. It operates cohesively, rather than as a fractured, flat picture created by a series of events.

Once success is achieved, document the process. It will help demonstrate the power of interdisciplinary teams that are focused on thinking like a customer when they're designing a product or service. Then let people copy what you've documented. Imitation is a fundamental basis of learning in all of us. Imitation also happens much more quickly. The actions of a relatively small number of passionate employees can dramatically shift the evolutionary future of a company in its journey to customer-centricity when their positive actions are praised and copied. The culture of your organization depends on communicating and sharing the successes of a few individuals (this is part of the storytelling that is so essential).

Accelerate the process by using this imitation concept – this copying – to foster even more change. Rather than drag your employees kicking and screaming into the new future, show them success through your participation in the process. You can cause imitation by intentionally modeling what you want to have happen and what you want to be imitated. It's the best kind of leadership because it defines

134

the transformational change while giving employees something to follow.

Becoming customer-centric is the new mandate for organizational success. You can talk for months and years about this different way of thinking, but the shortest distance between today and your new focus on customers is to give your company an example of how to do it by starting with one customer touch point. Real change is what resonates. When your employees see your sincerity and customer-directed leadership, old traditions and mindsets will melt away. Your 3D customer strategy will show everyone how you interpret customer focus and they will follow suit. After all, imitation is the sincerest form of flattery, isn't it?

SIX

The 3D System

All of life is an experiment.
The more experiments you make, the better.
Ralph Waldo Emerson

Customer 3D creates a dynamic system in which organizations empower all employees to be developers of valuable, creative ideas that are focused on customers. This is important, because the ability to generate ideas is an important component of a 3D organization's strategy. The 3D system encourages asking "what if" questions and using lateral thinking, which tends to be more creative and indirect than step-by-step thinking. It's a system that encourages employees to take things further in order to fully understand the customer's needs.

A system uses guidelines, but isn't so rigid that it's inflexible. NBA coach Phil Jackson's triangle offense is a system. The players know how the five teammates interact and have guidelines that influence how they operate in various game situations. But Jackson's system also provides enough flexibility that they can make individual judgments and produce the best approach to achieving their goals. Customer 3D puts organizations in a position to notice things they hadn't noticed before. In addition, the more passionate they are about becoming customer-centered, the more ideas they will develop.

One dictionary defines a system as an arrangement of things so related or connected that they form a unity or organic whole. The Customer 3D system links all of the component parts of an organization – people and functions – around a primary purpose: customer success. It forges the organizational components together so everything functions as a unit, just as the organs of the human body operate together. A system, of course, can be fluid and flexible.

The Potential Product

Nearly everything – products or services – can be enhanced to perform better than they do today. Envision the future potential of what you sell. The secret is to approach it from the user's viewpoint by thinking like a customer – and having a system in place that helps you implement your creative vision.

Harvard professor Ted Levitt defined this process for developing new products and services more than 40 years ago. He described four product categories:

- Generic: The minimum that gets you into the game
- Expected: The customer's minimal expectation for the product
- Augmented: Voluntary or unprompted improvements
- Potential: What's possible, what remains to be done

Augmentations, he said, were a way to provide product differentiation and to provide direction on the way to the ultimate "potential product." These positive adjustments change a customer's expectations and increase brand loyalty. Countless examples exist – adding wheels to luggage, for example.

The applications were always there – they were just waiting to be developed. Many times the solution is so obvious – after we see it, that is – that we wonder why someone didn't think of it sooner. Steve Jobs had this experience when he first saw the 1979 Alto computer created by Alan Kay. "I remember within 10 minutes of seeing the graphical user interface stuff, just knowing that every computer would work this way someday," Jobs said in *The Pixar Touch*.[1] "It was so obvious when you saw it."

The real genius of Levitt, however, was his recognition that there is always a potential product. Forward-thinking

138

companies operate under this "potential product" belief that there is always more they can offer customers. The successful examples are the ones in which the innovations rely on simple, focused solutions to real problems. Those companies are seen as ambitious because they're always asking, "What's new?"

Products and services are developed to take care of customers; high-performing organizations are founded on a culture and a discipline that continuously searches for better ways to deliver those products or services. These high performers have created a system in which employees focus on the same priorities because they are looking at those priorities from the customer's viewpoint.

The essence of this differentiation is not in individual tweaks to a product, but in how the entire creative system is managed to benefit the customer. Consider all of the items that were, until recent years, thought of as commodities – coffee, toothbrushes, chicken, beer, and small kitchen utensils, to name a few. How much was differentiation worth in terms of sales and profits when compared with selling a product or service that seemed destined to be a commodity? Based on today's variations in these product categories, differentiation must have significant value. And that value – and the profits that followed – were the result of a win-win relationship with customers.

Differentiation is possible everywhere when you look through the lens of the customer. 3D companies are never satisfied with the status quo. They enable the company's ability to design the ideal circumstances of the future around customer needs. Think about situations you've seen where companies moved closer to that potential product or service by thinking like a customer. How many examples can you name?

Never Stand Still
Innovation only happens when we ask the right questions – the ones our customers are asking. At some point, somebody must have asked, "Isn't there a better way than using a public address system to tell me my name is now at the top of the restaurant waiting list?" because that type of approach is less common than it used to be. In many 139

establishments, it's been replaced by electronic signaling technology that started out with one purpose in restaurants – notifying servers that their orders were ready – but ended up being used to assist both restaurant managers and customers. After this notification technology was applied to light-up discs given to waiting customers to alert them that it was their turn to be seated, more patrons stuck around when their name was added to a wait list instead of leaving. Clearly, applying existing technology to a new purpose improved business for the restaurants using it.

> There are no windows of opportunity (that will eventually shut) but infinite possibilities.
> *Margaret Wheatley and Myron Kellner-Rogers*

These "coaster" light-up pagers have changed the way restaurants manage their waiting lists, but cell phone pagers are the next technological evolution, as some restaurants now use a cell phone texting system to alert diners when their table is ready. It's less expensive for the restaurants and more convenient for the guests.

No organization can afford to stand still. The best way to avoid inertia is to think like a customer. Because innovation is on a continuum, companies must constantly evaluate where they are. Searching for these possibilities helps businesses learn how to sustain the energy they had when the company was founded.

Organizations need to invent, not just survive. Learn to experiment. Be inquisitive and willing to ask questions. Work is not a test in which you must fear making a mistake. Once you start, you won't want to stop. Margaret Wheatley and Myron Kellner-Rogers expressed it well in *A Simpler Way*: "The surprise within the surprise of every new discovery is that there is ever more to be discovered."[2]

Build a company with a culture that supports tinkering with existing systems to discover what's possible. Encourage teams to have "constant awareness" by asking these types of questions:

- How can we make this product or service more valuable to the customer?
- Are we evaluating each customer touch point by the same criteria that the customer uses?

- What transparency can we add to ensure that customers fully understand our processes?
- How might we better anticipate customer needs?

Don't lose your inquisitiveness when it comes to how you can improve. Your customers don't want you to stand still. They want you to pull them into the future with new ideas and services. That's why they're buying from you now and will rely on you in the future. Customers recognize that your organization's sense of discovery means you won't be the same as you were a year ago – you will be better. And that means *they* will be better.

In a 3D organization, every employee is trying to paint a masterpiece for customers. Continually experiment with the way work gets done for and by your customers. While creating better processes or products, you will also create loyal customers.

Barlean's Organic Oils generates new product ideas by listening to what customers and prospects tell them. For example, because the company produces, markets and sells nutritional oils, it hears a lot about oily taste, texture and appearance. Considering the product line, these are pretty tough objections to overcome. But the company was determined to do something about that, and, after three years of research and development, created a whole new category of nutritional oils. The "Omega-Swirl" line doesn't have the taste, look or texture of oil. Instead, it looks, tastes and feels like a fruit smoothie. The consumer and trade response to Omega-Swirl has been phenomenal, with the product winning several national industry awards. Herein lies the power of truly listening to your customers – and of tapping the subconscious mind with the power of questions. Consumers didn't ask specifically for Omega-Swirl, but it was a solution to their problems with the product category.

Customer Myopia
Imagine being forced to operate not as Barlean's does, but myopically, instead, with a very narrow view of what your customers needed: Quality, delivery, and low price. That's all you could address to keep customers satisfied. It doesn't take the world's biggest imagination to think of other things they might want – being easy to do business with, handling problems effectively when they arise, and

141

so on. The myopic limits are stifling, aren't they? They don't allow you to see the entire customer dynamic.

It's possible that your company sees things in a myopic way, too. How can you overcome this narrow view? Challenge members of your organization to list 100 things that customers might want. Encourage them to think big – what are other industries doing that might appeal to your customers? Review the lists for opportunities you can implement now – today! – to keep customers happy and loyal.

Most product-centric organizations rationalize that they know what customers need, so they focus mostly on how their products meet those minimum needs. What these companies perceive as needs, of course, fall far short of what customers want. Customer-centric organizations, on the other hand, look for new opportunities to offer their customers rather than waiting for them to be requested.

Customer 3D will expand your organization's field of vision so you're not myopic. Help your company realize that customers have many requirements that matter to them – and they expect your organization to be aware of them.

The First D in 3D is Discover

> Discovery consists of seeing what everybody has seen and thinking what nobody has thought.
> *Albert von Szent-Gyorgy*

The component of Customer 3D that requires generating ideas is based on, literally, three words beginning with D – discover, design and deliver.

Discovering a better way for customers begins with curiosity – your organization has to be curious about how it can do things better for customers. Once you're willing to explore and discover, you can find ways to innovate by improving existing processes and creating new products or services. People love the feeling that comes when they discover a better way to do something, and when 3D companies use discovery to provide higher value to customers, it energizes the entire organizational culture. The key is to be passionate about looking for – discovering – unmet customer needs.

At lubricant manufacturer WD-40 Company, the "Team Tomorrow" group in R&D focuses on discovering how it can make products "better than today." The team's innovations include a non-aerosol pump trigger created in response to legislation requiring cutbacks in aerosol storage in large factories. Testing with end-users told the company that customers liked it, but also that they preferred the pump to the aerosol because it gave them more control of the spray. In other words, they learned that control was a "white space" that they hadn't thought of as an opportunity. They will now consider this control component in designing and improving future products.

In the past, the top complaint regarding spray lubricant WD-40 was that users always lost the plastic straw that helped direct the spray out of the can's nozzle into a small area. Many end users sent the company examples of their own solutions for rigging the straw so that it wouldn't be misplaced – creating a way for the company to "discover" more about the problem. "Team Tomorrow" took the complaints seriously. They researched solutions, but every option was going to be expensive enough that the product would cost more. Team members were concerned that raising the price would cost them customers, but while working with test groups of end-users, they had another discovery: They had lost sight of the fact that "price" and "value" aren't the same thing. They moved forward with the best solution, the re-designed "Smart Straw," and while it costs more, it is a resounding success with customers, which translated into higher sales because of better value to the customer.

Company executive Graham Milner believes it's critical to observe how consumers actually use products. For example, families might tell researchers that they scrub their bathrooms once a week, but the reality is that they're often too busy to be as thorough as they'd like. Busy schedules mean that no matter what people say in focus groups, what they really want is the fastest and most convenient products and methods for bathroom cleaning. Organizations have to get out in the world, with cameras, to observe how the current products are used and discover the real needs of their end-users.

World-class performance requires a deep curiosity about how customer needs are shifting. Considering the speed with which change happens today, attracting and keeping customers requires

143

a significant rethinking of traditional management methods. To develop a customer-centered culture, you need constant, organization-wide efforts to discover and develop new information about customers. To stay ahead of the commodity trap, your company needs to be constantly learning about customer needs and how they are changing. If you are going to measure innovation (as we will show you in Chapter 7), you need to facilitate opportunities to happen.

One of the keys to develop this curiosity is to demonstrate best practices in helping customers. These examples will allow individual employees and departments to recognize their potential for improving customer value. Build the culture by using customer-related announcements at regular staff events, even coffee breaks, meals and start-of-the-day meetings. Make celebrations and awards for customer-centered behavior part of company ceremonies. Emphasize adding customer value at training sessions. Set aside a room or area where prototypes are displayed and discussed. Do technological research to spot trends that could be used inside your company. Envision every creative idea as a model for the future.

Having access to outside-the-organization customer perspectives is a fundamental success factor for 3D companies. Asking lots of questions will yield plenty of new information that can be used to address customer needs, leading to the anticipation of solutions before customers even ask for them. The end result of this culture of curiosity is organizational flexibility. By focusing on customers as the center of activity, all elements within the organization become aligned to adapt to customer needs.

The passive, more slowly paced reactions of the past no longer work. If your organization's sense of discovery has waned, find a solution that will jump-start its passion for serving customers again. Have contests for best research leading to a customer-centered innovation. Systematically distribute articles that reinforce the 3D position. Develop topics of conversations for the customer that will generate useful information for possible innovations. Customer-centricity will not happen unless your organization is curious about customers and what they will need in the future. If you want your company to be customer-centered, create a culture that is continuously looking for

144

ways to learn more about customers. Don't become complacent. Be an explorer.

Unmet Customer Needs

Where do the truly creative, market-changing ideas come from? They develop from an environment inside the organization that allows them to germinate and blossom – a creative, customer-centered culture. 3D organizations share a leadership strategy committed to the belief that designing from the viewpoint of the customer will strengthen what the organization will offer.

Target, the discount retailer, transformed its organization by using its discovery of unmet customer needs to design innovative solutions that gave them a competitive advantage. For example, the retailer bought the patent to the Clear Rx™ medicine bottle because it was intuitive, and therefore safer, for the consumer. The unique packaging includes personalized neck rings for each family member along with clear and simple labels with larger type. After using these bottles, some customers switched to Target's pharmacy exclusively for prescriptions. How versatile is your organization in defining "unmet customer needs" broadly enough to discover improvements which your customers will value?

Kathie Dengler, senior vice president for guest and institutional services at The Strong, says, "It's all about listening to the guest. When a cleaning staff employee overheard a guest say that she only had a $20 bill and no change for the vending machines, he told the gift shop manager, who took change from the till to the guest. The guest was amazed because she didn't realize that anyone knew about her dilemma." She adds that employees are taught to "own" a guest. If they aren't able to handle a question or problem, they will walk the guest to another host, explain the problem, and make sure that second host will handle it from that point forward.

Extraordinary

There is a simple method for encouraging breakthrough thinking that helps your business grow: Observe those processes or outcomes for customers that you know you can do better than your competitors. Every process that touches your customers represents an opportunity to distinguish your organization as better. Here's how

145

you can identify these opportunities using three categories that your customers will use to describe your processes:

- **Poor:** Ugly, supplier-centric procedures that make your customers wonder why they are buying from your company.
- **Ordinary:** These interfaces make you look the same as your competition. They are just average.
- **Extraordinary:** When a process is truly better, customers respond with delight. It's unique and compelling to both employees and customers.

> Everything I've ever done was out of fear of being mediocre.
> *Chet Atkins*

Ask your staff to describe several of your processes and argue in favor of the adjectives they use. It's critical that they approach the task from the customer's viewpoint. They should say, "The customer sees this event (your ordering process, for example) as (for example) cumbersome/ the same as our competitor's process/very user-friendly." It should be somewhere on a continuum of poor to extraordinary.

Deal with your really weak areas immediately. Most of your touch points, however, will fall into the "ordinary" category. But you want them to be better than your competition, don't you? Take these up to "extraordinary" by making them easier or more enjoyable for your customers. At the extraordinary level, work on function, not fashion. Enlist all employees to help rethink how your organization creates value in process, not product. Put yourself in your customer's shoes and ask why your organization continues to perpetuate processes that are not customer-focused. The areas that need streamlining will become obvious; they will catalyze your efforts to turn average into remarkable.

Nurture a culture that believes you can improve everything. (Yes, everything!) Challenge your team to become better than your competitors. Don't stop at one or two changes, though. Model every innovation that takes you further. Crystallize new ideas around customer impact.

Don't be intimidated by the misconception that creativity requires special powers. It doesn't. We just need to welcome change and be motivated to question every process, looking for ways to improve it or speed it up. Creativity is often more about seeing the "same old, same old" from a fresh perspective – in this case, the customer's – than it is about having some type of innate gift. When we think like our customers, we begin to see illogical and complex steps that can be changed in every service that our organization provides.

Before undertaking any new initiative, we should define what a great outcome would look like. The Customer 3D system teaches organizations to ask, "What's the point of the exercise?" or "What are we trying to achieve?" as we undertake the change. When the answer involves a clear understanding of the customer benefits, your team will have clarity. During this early definition stage, 3D performers know how to engage customers in genuine conversations and to back up this sincere interest with an ability to listen and respond.

With a clear definition of your destination, you will know when you have arrived at it. Hammering out this definition early in the process can be uncomfortable work, but when your customer is central to that final destination, you are better able to focus your efforts.

Training for Creativity That Focuses on Customers

A number of creative techniques help us visualize new ideas for customers. They "shake up" the status quo and jumpstart the innovation process. Lisa Aschmann's *1000 Songwriting Ideas*[3] is an excellent resource for creativity exercises. Her compendium of creative premises for songs should trigger more than enough ideas within your organization. Here are two examples:

- **Idea #922:** Complete the first part of this sentence, *"... and nobody objected."* If you focus your answer on how you can help your customers and nobody objected to the solutions, shouldn't you implement them? For example, "We switched to a no-questions-asked returns policy...and nobody objected." Now, develop these ideas into a song with several verses and how your customers would react. Let a group of your colleagues analyze the song's ideas and actually expand them into some simulations of things your customers will like. Sounds like fun to me – and beneficial, as well.

- **Idea #713:** Imagine yourself in a club before the band is

147

going to play your tune. Introduce the song by talking about some aspect of its premise (customer-related, of course) without identifying the title before it's performed. How about, "This song tells the story of a change that a service business (name your company) made that ended up making life unbelievably easier for its customers." Then, expand on how this idea replaced a more traditional system and how the customers thanked your company for the innovation. It could be the source of some very creative changes that your customers will love – and you get to role play as the "performer" introducing your song.

Aschmann has created some extraordinarily clever ways to help us become more open-minded – to find what she calls our "beginner mind." You don't have to be musical, although you might learn that you are more musical than you give yourself credit for. Her book helps us see that music will help us overcome our fear of rejection and open the floodgates of inspiration. I encourage you to experiment with some of her scenarios. They will help your organization overcome self-imposed limitations so that you can do great things for your customers.

Look at How Customers Act

These days, we have to think expansively about what customers really want when they buy from us. The product or service you offer can no longer be looked at as satisfying the narrow space it was created for. Discovery happens in an anthropological way when observing customers, which can lead to breakthrough opportunities. McDonalds offers a good example. When the fast food restaurant chain wanted to improve the quality of its milkshakes, almost all of the researchers focused on just the product. Should the new version be sweeter, thicker or colder? But one of the researchers chose to study the customers themselves, discovering that milkshakes were purchased early in the day, during the traditional breakfast time.

It turns out that the breakfast shake-drinkers were commuters who drank them in the car because they could do it with one hand and without making a mess. The researchers were about to overlook this dimension because of what author Clay Shirky calls "milkshake mistakes."[4] First, they concentrated only on the product attributes and assumed they knew everything about why customers were

148

purchasing it. Secondly, they took a narrow view of the market – in this case, the type of food people typically eat in the morning.

Most companies believe they know what the market needs. Customers will either buy it or they won't. But customers – not you – are your best idea sources, if you allow them to be. All it takes is observing and changing what you do based on what you discover. Ask yourself, "Why does the customer use our product or service?" But don't make the "milkshake mistake" of thinking of just the product attributes, without regard to what role the customers want it to play for them. Jane Fulton Suri of design firm IDEO explains it this way: "Observation forces us to focus on the actions that we are trying to support through design, rather than the things we will ultimately produce."[5]

Products don't exist in isolation with narrow uses anymore. The milkshake mistake is a good illustration of why you don't want to be product-centric. When you're customer-centric, you are positioned to notice things you hadn't before, and the outcome will be better for customers. Your creativity increases, as does your ability to proactively design new ideas for those customers.

No More Status Quo

Creativity helps elevate our organizations above the status quo, which is comforting and familiar, of course. In many cases, we're lulled into accepting what exists without realizing how much better it could be. While we don't always need to change the status quo, we do need to challenge it. Customer-centered organizations excel at challenging the status quo on behalf of customers.

Status quo can be dangerous. The danger, of course, from a supplier's standpoint is that your expectations about what the customer wants are too low. It's easy to think that customers simply want what you have been giving them all along. So, while the status quo can provide consistency, it can also create inertia. Creative organizations get beyond these assumptions that hide the need to find solutions. They have taught themselves to recognize that they will find other choices, but they have to look for them.

Wilson Sporting Goods changed one market completely by looking

149

at a taken-for-granted product differently. For decades, Little League baseball players were stuck wearing oversized plastic bucket helmets that didn't seem to fit anyone quite right. The clumsy helmet provided little or no protection, so safety was a myth. Wilson re-entered this market with a well-researched alternative that not only worked much better, but was also considered cool by the players. Within three years, Wilson's market share rose from 0 to 30 percent.

Use the batting helmet success as a metaphor for customer-centered improvements in your company. If somebody had been paying attention through years of Little League baseball, we would have had better helmets sooner. The market wanted something different, but manufacturers and customers simply accepted what they already had. So what's the lesson for any organization that wants to overcome inertia in its thinking? Focus on customer actions, not what you're producing. Understand the unexpressed needs of the people you are serving by thinking like a customer. Like the improved batting helmet, there are better ideas out there just waiting to be discovered.

Start noticing things. Systematically identify what hasn't changed or evolved in the customer experience and question why. Turn over a few rocks by asking how your organization can transform taken-for-granted features into those that excite and add value. Look for evidence that you are improving. The more enthusiastic you are about helping customers, the more likely it is that you'll get meaningful results.

The Staples Singers sang "I'll Take You There;" that's what every organization should do for its customers. Traditional companies change what isn't working when the change leads to an outcome that's better for them; customer-centric organizations change what's already working because it's better for the customer.

The Second D in 3D is Design

Customer 3D is based on design thinking, which makes us attentive, like a good designer, and helps us let go of pre-existing ideas. The Customer 3D system guides your organization as it connects seemingly unrelated ideas or processes. Ambiguity in business disappears because a 3D approach clears the mind of clutter and lets us focus on what the customer will value. Customer-centered thinking is the nexus that positions customers at the center of a situation or process and connects them with the business as a whole. Breakthrough ideas that come through the first D – discovery – are easier to identify than ever before.

During the past 25 years, Six Sigma and other approaches have encouraged businesses to standardize products and reduce the number of variations. This direction is acceptable in a company-centric world where internal process

> Design is so critical it should be on the agenda of every meeting in every single department.
> *Tom Peters*

efficiencies are all that matter. But this strategy amounts to ratcheting down of existing systems, not designing new ones.

What's needed, instead, is an open attitude toward designing customer-centered innovations. There are many impressive stories of organizations that developed new markets by giving customers more positive experiences that were driven by the customer-centered insights of designers. The Coaster bike is a great example of how this works. When Shimano, a Japanese manufacturer of bicycle components, was faced with less growth in its high-end racing and mountain bikes, it used design techniques to create a market for baby-boomers where virtually none existed before.

The company's research with non-customers revealed that many adults were intimidated by the prospect of purchasing a bike. They had become too complex, and the cost of maintaining them seemed odd when compared with the bikes of their youth. They were also concerned about safety while cycling on roads that were not bicycle-friendly. Shimano responded to the market research by designing Coaster bikes, with no controls on the handlebars because riders would brake by backpedaling and no gear shifting cables around the frame because an onboard computer shifted the three gears automatically.

What's most remarkable about this story is that while the new bike was designed by a components supplier, the innovative bikes were manufactured by conventional bicycle companies. The first year, three manufacturers came on board. Five years later, there were 10. These bicycle manufacturers design their own versions. The process was systematic but creative, structured around a customer-centered requirement to deliver the least negative impact on the customer and the greatest benefit. This openness to new design ideas almost always results in game-changing developments that make it easy for customers to shift to an outcome that provides them with better value.

What are the characteristics that you want in your organization and its teams? They probably include:

- Creativity
- Planning excellence
- Ability to be intuitive
- Willingness to take risks
- Curiosity
- Vision
- Discipline

Aren't these the traits you typically find in a designer? Designers know how to reach people – your customers. They see things differently. Designers fully understand what exists in an industry or an organization and they push it forward or stretch it to make it better for the customer. They bring an interdisciplinary approach that solves existing problems and innovates for the future. Customer 3D teaches all employees to participate in design intuitively.

At Microsoft, Principal Learning and Development Solutions Manager Tonya Peck is responsible for supporting the learning and development of a staff of 35,000 engineers. Her goal is to foster knowledge exchange because the way engineers learn is changing. In the past, for example, a central portal of information was sufficient. Now, it is more social, with engineering employees looking both externally and internally for knowledge. They use a variety of methods to find answers to a range of questions. Part of Peck's work involved designing an "Answers" portal in which engineers could ask questions and "we will find out for them." When a question is answered, however, the group evaluates it to determine whether to revise it. In the software industry, "solutions are like a layer cake." They are built in layers rather than created as a stand-alone answer.

Holograms. The hologram was accidentally discovered in 1947 while scientist Dennis Gabor was working to improve the electron microscope. However, holograms were not utilized until the 1960's with the invention of the laser, which provided the purer, more intense light that was necessary to create useful holograms. Today, embracing the spirit of Ted Levitt's potential product concept, holography has produced thousands of new products, including 3D models to aid surgical planning or forensic science investigations, holographic data storage and retrieval, and improved supermarket scanners.

List as many adjectives ending in '-er' – such as better, brighter, faster, smaller, etc. – that could be associated with your products. Using thinking-like-a-customer techniques, imagine how creative variations of your products (such as Barlean's better-tasting fish oils) would provide innovative, more enjoyable solutions for your customers.
Figure 6.1

National Geographic, December 1988

Microsoft is employing more design thinking in its innovation process. The Office ribbon in Microsoft Office 2007, for example, has totally changed the interaction model for customers. The engineers used a combination of building on the past – and understanding how customers used previous versions – with empowering the team to do the right thing for customer. It was, Peck says, all about "how to make it more productive for the customer."

The designers took a leap of faith that reformatting tasks on the ribbon would result in a much shorter learning curve for individuals. In addition, they removed tasks used by less than 2 percent of users. They used a problem definition technique to think beyond the previous systems and to leverage the intuition of customers. The more attractive Office 2007 design was validated as more understandable by customers. It was more proactive than the path in

153

the past, which had seen more incremental changes in each updated version of Office. This type of design thinking is being used for the Windows phone, which is taking an equally proactive consumer direction.

Peck says, "Everything is moving to a services model and the evolution of what that means is the big buzz." Like every 3D organization, Microsoft has its finger on the pulse of the customer community. With every iteration, it is becoming more agile and experimental. Peck refers to service design as "being in perpetual beta." Every 3D organization operates this way for its customers.

Similarly, WEIDMANN Electrical Technology, Inc. began to work closely with engineers at specific clients to make their transformers less costly and more efficient. As part of this process, it began working with companies that repaired insulation components. These service providers typically didn't have on-site engineering capabilities and were simply duplicating the insulation components they were replacing. WEIDMANN took its design services to these repair shops and showed them how to put transformers back together so they were almost better than when they were new, using modern tools. The value of WEIDMANN's upgrades allowed the repair shop customers to test their repaired transformers at 100 percent of the expected voltage level, rather than at 70 percent, because of the new design technology that WEIDMANN introduced.

This close-to-the-customer process has provided WEIDMANN with a deeper, 3D definition of value from the customer's perspective. They could see problems before, but didn't fully understand what the customer actually valued. Now, the company's team of engineers looking at the customer's complete experience and asking, "What can we do better for them?"

Train your organization to use its design capabilities in conjunction with developing the solutions that will add value to customers' businesses. Designer thinking means emerging thinking and will become more and more important in your partnerships with customers. It's driven by the desire to make customer experiences better. It's the source of true organic growth that starts with focusing on how an organization's existing capabilities can be designed to improve customer experiences.

154

3D Printing. The speed at which 3D printers have become cost effective is remarkable. These printers create objects by forming and hardening one layer of material (generally metal or plastic) on top of another until a three-dimensional object has been built from a flat print or drawing. Today, 3D printers dramatically shorten the production time for a number of products on the market today. They are also creating completely new and/or industries, such as designer prosthetics, parts for antiques cars, and even home building. Instead of a top-secret process only known by governments and big manufacturers, 3D printing has become more customer-centered by moving the design process much closer to consumers.

How can your organization create a better product by focusing on customers' needs and adding new dimensions that customers will value?

The Third D in 3D is Deliver

The Customer 3D system makes sure the organization delivers the better solutions that have been identified as opportunities for customers. It facilitates the design-to-delivery process and strengthens core competencies.

It requires a structured system. WD-40's process involves compiling and prioritizing the most customer-centered ideas. They take the top 10 from a list of more than 40 being considered at a given time. To prioritize, they take into account a number of considerations, including changes in government regulations, competitive response, the size of the brand, and perceived opportunity. When a specific innovation is more important in several markets, the delivery process is focused on that concept because it will yield a greater impact to customers.

At WEIDMANN, the Joint Engineering Cost Reduction Team has focused on customer needs to deliver several new products, including a new insulation material that dries 30 percent faster than traditional insulation and has other industry-specific attributes. In addition, it increases customer manufacturing throughput by 30 percent and makes it possible to build smaller, more efficient transformers. This

155

increase in efficiency was available before the 2010 Department of Energy efficiency regulations made it a requirement, and allowed redesigned transformers to meet those requirements without adding copper, which would have been more expensive.

Delivery can also include better ways to carry out the physical delivery of the product or service. WEIDMANN, for example, also has a dedicated logistics team that keeps inventory at six service centers around the U.S. so customers never have to worry about out-of-stock situations. When Hurricane Katrina hit the Gulf Coast in 2004, the company had enough products in stock to keep customers operating immediately after the storm.

But the success of these service centers led to even greater innovations for their customers. Todd Thiele, vice-president of sales, noted, "The implementation of our Service Centers created enough value with our customers that we decided to re-organize with a dedicated Logistics department as opposed to just a function that falls under our Customer Service department. The newly formed Logistics Group is sanctioned to manage the entire supply chain of WEIDMANN's products including the traditional freight and warehousing functions." More importantly, however, the Logistics Group took on the added role of pro-actively interpreting customers' material replenishment reports. The department focuses on ensuring an adequate supply of insulation material throughout the year and especially during the peak transformer demand in the summer months. Thiele continued, "This model worked so well that one customer actually approached us to see if the Logistics Group could manage all of their transformer commodity products, including those from our competitors."

"Deliver" also refers to learning to deliver fun as part of your culture. Employees in 3D organizations get to add their own twist to company activities so they are more fun for customers. Because having fun is an important part of the culture at Barlean's Organic Oils, the company is always looking for ways to make customers smile or get them more involved. For example, one employee worked with a local bartender to develop alcoholic beverage recipes using the company's Omega-3 oils. Barlean's tested several at a private party at an industry trade show, using the feedback to select

156

one drink to sample at the company's show booth as part of its 20th anniversary celebration. In addition, customer-submitted videos on the company's website make both employees and other customers smile (especially the video showing children begging their mother to let them have Omega Swirl as a treat because they love the taste so much).

Creating Customer-Centered Ideas

It's also important to deliver a more positive energy in your relationships with customers through creativity. Try invigorating old ideas by framing them around the customer. Customer-centric leaders continually experiment with the way work gets done for and by their customers. One of the best ways to develop the ability to do this is by establishing a dedicated time of the week for teams to generate new ideas. Corning's Sullivan Park R&D lab in Corning, NY, allowed employees to spend 10 percent of their time on "Friday afternoon experiments" to develop off-beat ideas in experimental glass. One of these experiments, a mainstream idea rejected by the head of research, became a new technology business after it was pursued as a Friday experiment.

> Every now and then a man's mind is stretched by a new idea or sensation, and never shrinks back to its former dimensions.
> *Oliver Wendell Holmes, Sr.*

Creativity is rarely a company's primary activity. But it's the activity that will make the biggest difference in your future if it's focused on the customer. Creativity helps overcome a narrow-minded attitude that makes customers uncomfortable. Put aside concerns about the return on investment initially so that you can freely develop ideas that will create something better for your customers. Don't worry about failures; inaction is the worst kind of failure.

There are paybacks, of course, for your business. Creativity generates its power at the practical level with new products and services that will make a difference for customers. It also helps customers form a positive impression of your organization, which influences the long-term customer experience. At subscription management company cSubs, employees are encouraged to always think creatively about the possibilities for clients. Departments hold

157

meetings designed to help them better understand client needs; they have permission to find creative ways, when necessary, to meet those needs. Because of this fresh approach to being customer-centered, cSubs was selected as a recipient of the 2010 Alfred P. Sloan Awards for Business Excellence in Workplace Flexibility in the at-large category.

As you create new customer-centered ideas, you create lots of loyal customers. Committing to creativity that will benefit your customers is the greatest improvement you can accomplish in the next 12 months. Both internally and externally, creativity is enriching, energizing and profitable.

The methods used to develop new ideas for customers have not changed much over the years. James Webb Young was one of the first business writers to define an idea as "a new combination of facts." In *A Technique for Producing New Ideas*, he noted that success with generating innovative thinking becomes stronger when our "ability to make new combinations is heightened by our ability to see relationships."[6]

Young compares the idea-searching process to what occurs in a kaleidoscope. When viewed through a prism, the pieces of colored glass in this toy are seen as geometrical designs. Every turn of a kaleidoscope's cylinder shifts these bits of glass into new patterns. The more pieces of glass, the more possibilities there are for new and exciting combinations. The same possibilities exist for customer-centered ideas in all organizations. Teams that bring together people with a variety of experiences will have the most potential to develop fresher ideas within our organizations.

Too often, we mistakenly believe that ideas that will benefit customers will arrive magically, so "we sit around, hoping for inspiration to strike us." Young shows us that new combinations develop through persistence and use of a systematic method. As he observes, "this (idea-generating) technique can consciously be cultivated." He suggests using a formal process for documenting specific information, which can be synthesized or digested when searching for new ideas.

158

Customer 3D organizations have product development systems in place that are based on observing and listening to customers. These internal systems help them respond quickly to changes in the customer environment and to keep the company customer-centered. Barlean's, for example, keeps a log of customer ideas which they call "SWOT," with more than 10,000 feedback comments. "We look for patterns and trends and are continually looking for opportunities that will benefit the customer," says Scott North, director of customer service.

Customer service personnel are encouraged to add feedback to the SWOT system as often as possible – at least five entries per day – describing customer comments or questions that would help improve Barlean's products or processes. The thinking is that for every one customer who reports something, there might be 10 who experience something similar but don't report it. For example, the company used to sell its Omega Swirls products only in a 16-ounce size but because there were customer comments about how smaller sizes would be helpful, the company eventually introduced 12-ounce and 8-ounce sizes.

Process improvements for customers are driven by this computer system and portal. Employees are allowed and encouraged to do open-ended updates to processes on the system. For example, Sarah Willett customer ambassador, notes that "If I did the research about the dimensions of a product piece, I would share that information on the computer system for everyone to use. It's like a wiki, and works better than sending e-mail messages that might get lost. I simply go into that product, note the updates, and share my findings."

Ideas at 3D organizations most often happen through a systematic and collaborative process. Customer 3D is a system of co-creation that extends throughout an organization to develop innovative customer-centered ideas. Our ability to combine our experiences and direct them to improvements on behalf of our customers is essential to customer-centricity. Like a kaleidoscope, the more facets that we consider, the richer the opportunities for those customers. However, we can't forget that generating new ideas involves using a technique that we have to work at.

Organizations that want to develop an effective process for designing new, customer-centered solutions need to educate teams of employees to make the most of ideas and encounters they have experienced. It starts with establishing the organization's unique capabilities for innovative thinking, based on historical successes, and it opens the idea-development process to all employees, with the only constraint being that ideas must be justified based on value to customers. When they embrace the fun and complexity of patterns and relationships, as in a kaleidoscope, employees feel more comfortable about unleashing their creativity to benefit their customers.

Make the Exception the Rule

Every organization today is faced with figuring out how to be better than its competitors. Success with innovation, however, begins with the right mindset. If you believe that your new idea or creation is an exception to the status quo, embrace its disruptive benefits. Think about how it can become standard for all of your customers. When the new concept proves better than before, its success pulls ordinary performances up to a new level. Innovation thrives in cultures that are comfortable with making the exception the rule.

3D customer-centricity is built around incremental changes on behalf of customers. It involves designing logical improvements to what already exists. It nudges the current state forward to become a better version of the product or process, delivering higher value to the customer while the customer performs the same action as before. The E-ZPass RFID system in the Northeast U.S. is a good example. E-ZPass uses a small device in the owner's car to pay the driver's tolls electronically, reduce waiting times at toll booths. Drivers are still paying their tolls, of course, but the process is significantly easier and more convenient than stopping at every toll booth.

Most innovations fall into the "incremental change" category because those are easier to envision. We can readily visualize the "what-if" results of a new feature being added to an existing product or service. Incremental change is built on the premise that every product or service has the potential to be better in the future. Customers will value the change, even if they don't all choose to participate. Not all toll road drivers use E-ZPass, for example, but the

160

benefits for the ones who do take advantage of it are worth it.

3D innovation also happens in even bigger ways when, rather than tweaking an existing product or service, companies develop new ideas that represent breakthrough performance instead. These breakthrough ideas have to be iconic – big ideas and deployment strategies are necessary. With a high-impact idea and some corporate financial help, Common Ground renovated the Times Square Hotel into a model for change for hundreds of homeless New Yorkers and transformed the neighborhood. The effort proved not only that the project would work, but that a not-for-profit organization could help the homeless for one-third the per person cost being spent by city services.

The Common Ground prototype demonstrated to naysayers that the idea was doable, with a high chance of success. In *Rules of Thumb*, Alan Webber summarizes what's needed: "The job of an iconic project is to make change believable."[7] The lesson is that big ideas can start with a demonstration model that proves the viability of a strategy. "Once people can see it, feel it, and benefit from it, then change isn't an abstraction. It's real," he writes.

Innovation happens when organizations think like their customers. The decision to choose incremental change versus transformational change depends largely on the investment and degree of difficulty involved. But in both categories, the undertaking should be grounded in a belief that it's okay to make the exception the rule. Organizations should constantly be looking for a better way to accomplish what they want to do for the customer.

Art or Science?

Customers identify with organizations that are less concerned with rules and more interested in being flexible and mindful of individual needs. High-level customer-centricity is driven more by art than science. 1D organizations rely on authoritarian control because they worry about being left vulnerable by ambiguity and a lack of rules. 3D customer-centering loves flexibility and believes that doing what's right for the customer outweighs the artificiality of rules. Because of customer individuality and needs in specific situations, rules and procedures become burdensome to employees dealing with diverse customer types. 1D transactional performance requires more science. Connecting with customers at the more advanced 3D level must be humanistic, designed to create fresh ideas for customers, so it requires a more artful approach.

3D suppliers believe in providing customers with high quality and distinctive products and services that customers value. Erring on the side of the traditional scientific approach, 1D organizations tend to impose rules that spell out what to do in every possible circumstance as their remedy for all customer interfaces. Rote performance, however, will no longer satisfy today's customers, who expect greater responsiveness.

Ritz-Carlton realized the need to re-orient its approach a few years ago. After decades of asking employees to follow a 20-point list of customer service basics, they shifted to a simpler 12-point set of values that allowed employees to use their judgment and improvise. The new approach encouraged staff to sense customer needs and act accordingly. Tightly defined actions, such as "always carry a guest's luggage" shifted to value statements such as, "I am empowered to create unique, memorable, and personal experiences for our guests." As a result, customer satisfaction improved.

Rules-driven operations, of course, are necessary for support or backroom services that function best with no variation. Here, standardization brings control and reduces process errors. These business areas assume that customer needs are completely known and the methods for taking care of them can be standardized. Examples include packing and shipping, or manufacturing, where a process must be repeated again and again with consistent quality. All companies have these types of functional activities that can be evaluated according to internal measures, which means there are some roles that should be formulaic and designed to reduce variation.

The culture at The Strong works with just one rule: Safety first. Everything else is flexible. The motto, Dengler says, is "People first, things second. At the end of the day, our employees are not parrots. We want to let their personality come through and give them the latitude to interact with guests and to judge each guest's emotional level."

The organization wants to help create lasting memories. A grandparent, for example, said he had taught each of his grandchildren to play chess at the exhibit in the museum. Another family watched their disabled 5-year-old girl hold onto a shopping cart and walk for the first time in her life at the Wegmans Super Kids Market exhibit. The museum has been the site of many wedding proposals.

Being customer-centered demands a system that thrives on creativity and more personalized results. It is built off of the ability to recognize customer cues and to proactively respond to customer needs. For example, when a child started bleeding, his mother got blood on her blouse. One of the hosts gave her a new Strong T-shirt from the gift shop, which saved the day for the family. That behavior is instilled into the culture that teaches the hosts to react positively to customers' needs. The result: happier customers with fewer rules for the staff to enforce. Dengler commented, "It's amazing the appreciation that we receive."

3D organizations have moved their companies away from a one-size-fits-all approach. They are differentiating themselves by developing the art of maximizing customer value, which involves creating outcomes that rely on customer-driven, rather than rules-driven, measures of success.

3D organizations are adept at seeing the many opportunities to develop cool, new ideas for their customers because they are not confined, as most 1D organizations are, to the traditional view of their industry. 3D companies are open to the art of exploring these no-limits ideas. To advance customer-centricity, they expand their views of what is possible. They move from analytical, industry-specific approaches to a deeper understanding of products and processes by using a synthesis of ideas generated from other disciplines.

When knowledge is integrated, they see everything more fully. This open-ended thinking exposes the many dimensions of the experience that customers encounter. It's a synthesis that will help 3D organizations implement unique ideas faster than their competition.

Great performance for customers, therefore, requires a mix of art   163 and science. Science creates efficiencies in the basic processes that need to be close to error-free. Art takes performance beyond the ordinary to a higher level of customer-centricity that customers love and value. Success happens when organizations develop an understanding of customer needs and learn how to act with freedom and agility to design an outcome that customers value. Customer needs are changing more rapidly than ever before and we must acknowledge that taking care of those aspirations will depend more on art than science to remain extraordinary.

An organization's journey to 3D for its customers is never complete. Organizations that use the Customer 3D system start with the belief that they can always make their products and processes better and more valuable for customers. Their journey through the process involves making variations and re-combinations that expand their customer relationships in ways that deliver improvements for those customers. The journey deepens the customers' perspectives of the business and builds the 3D organization's reputation as an original.

Characteristics That Protect 3D Organizations from Being Copied

3D organizations make it difficult for the competition to copy them if those competitors are using 1D traditional, product-centered performances. 3D companies:

- Always set higher performance goals because, although they are already successful, they are hungry to improve
- Commit to a strong customer strategy, which balances their operational and financial strategies.
- Empower all employees to be solutions-finders in ways that make customers feel like they're working with their own consultant
- Constantly carry out the detective work to discover underserved customer needs
- Study the techniques of other highly customer-centered companies
- Answer all questions about how they can improve from the customer's viewpoint
- Embrace change and manage it by thinking like a customer
- Set the standards for their industries because they are never satisfied until customers are asking competitors whether they are "doing it like (their company name) does it"

PART III

You've Got to Admit, It's Getting Better: How Customer-Centered Organizations Keep Improving

There are assumptions you hold
and assumptions that have a hold on you.
Harvard Professor Robert Kegan, Ph.D.

A 3D organization is an idea, not a building or a quarterly earnings report. It is a commitment to take the traditional corporate culture to a new dimension by using customer-centricity as the most distinguishing trait of the organization. It adds depth, tangibility and solidity to every performance; this delivers much greater authenticity to the customer.

1D organizations are stuck in a paradigm of event-driven transactions. Building on this thinking, 2D organizations try to create a series of customer experiences through stand-alone performances which they hope will be pleasing for individual customers. 3D goes beyond to design and deliver a customer experience that is universal throughout the organization – one that is cultural and that is cumulative.

To make certain your new customer-centered thinking approach is effective, you need a monitoring system – not a rigid measurement system, just indicators that will help keep your organization expanding into a more fully developed dimension. These indicators sustain your new-found tendency to stretch and remain flexible –

167

traits that are ingrained in the 3D business model.

On your journey to becoming customer-centric, you'll see that what we call "life" or wholeness in a company's culture is a general, measurable condition that exists in every part of the company. It can be formulated precisely through activities that will create positive changes that customers will care about. Trending – monitoring the progress – is an important way to reinforce that momentum is still happening in the organization.

SEVEN

The Customer 3D™ Index:
Measuring Customer Centeredness

Execution... refers to the way that people,
working together in an organizational setting,
mobilize resources to deliver on the strategy.
Phil Rosenzweig, from The Halo Effect

Sustaining customer-centricity requires a navigation system and a focus on key milestones to help organizations understand their progress. Every 3D organization needs to know how effectively it is executing its customer strategy. That is why the Customer 3D system uses simple, clear metrics that measure the fundamental components of 3D performance.

1D customer performance is average, ordinary, and focuses on the product or service that your organization offers. Some product-centered companies with motivated employees have reached 2D performance, which is great individual service at the transactional level. Employees are courteous and helpful to customers, but within the constraints of their product-centered rules and procedures. The customer is pleased, but these employee actions, however, are still delivered to individual customers on a reactive basis. 3D expands beyond this to add value for customers throughout the organization.

Many one-dimensional organizations look at 3D companies and say to themselves, "They're so lucky." On the contrary, luck has nothing to do with it. In reality, 3D businesses have leaders who have:

169

- Catalyzed a strong culture
- Set clear, customer-centered goals
- Ensured that the organization works hard to reach those goals

Customer-centricity will never fully happen, however, unless the new behavior is measured. The Customer 3D Index measures the gaps between reactive behaviors in response to customers and delivering an exceptional, proactive strategy for customers across the organization. It complements the basic customer satisfaction indicators used in standard research by focusing the organization on its performance beyond the break-even point with customers. It measures your aptitude for staying competitive by monitoring your organization's customer readiness and ability to be proactive.

20th Century business leaders were obsessed with mechanistic management philosophies that worked on parts of a business as if they were machine components. In contrast with these mechanistic views, 3D organizations don't have a lot of "moving parts." There are many employees, of course, but the approach is one of flow rather than parts.

Today, game-changing 3D companies are leading the transition from a stolid, product-centered world to one with fluency and customer-centered innovation. They understand that success isn't about working narrowly on methods; rather, it's about opening up a wide range of possibilities by delivering extraordinary results for customers.

3D organizations have created a dynamic "outside-in" culture by educating the entire workforce about what it means to be customer-centric and how to deliver the necessary elements in their performances. The elements within the organization include:

- Structured techniques for empowering employees, including providing parameters for making decisions to take care of customers
- A dynamic communication system within the organization so that boundaries between departments and facilities are more permeable
- A clear system of customer "ownership"
- A process for sharing great performances stories of customer-centered behavior throughout the organization

- A clear definition of what customers consider "value" versus "non-value"

The move from 1D to 3D is driven by a sense of possibility. The Customer 3D Index captures and reinforces the behaviors that will continue to move the organization into that new dimension. Success is based on proving to customers that you not only care about the same things they do, but that you also care about making what you do for them work better. In order to move to a 3D state, you must measure business performance by three simple scorecard factors that best represent the deployment of the 3D customer strategy. These elements are generating ideas, permeability, and culture.

You Need to Hear the Voice of the Customer

All thriving organizations that are passionate about becoming 3D start with a basic measure of their customer satisfaction. This feedback process captures and measures the voice-of-the-customer (VOC) perceptions to determine how well the company performs with basic product and service quality, when handling problems, and with getting the customer to the "break even" point. Most well-managed organizations already have this measurement process in place, which provides a satisfaction index that evaluates performance against customer expectations. It assesses what customers think of their experiences with the organization. Factors that are typically considered for this basic feedback exercise include (but aren't limited to):

- Customers' satisfaction with your organization's performance against fixed standards, such as order accuracy and fulfillment, along with other processes the organization must get right for customers to be satisfied and loyal
- Problem solving and critical incident handling
- Customer-focused metrics, including customer perceptions of how responsive and easy to do business with the organization is – overall and by department
- Observations of customers using your products in the field

Unfortunately, satisfaction surveys covering topics such as these have a bad reputation because very little is ever done with them. Why is that? Because the results can't be acted on.

But you can change that. There are many variations of home-grown   171 surveys created by internal teams and offered to customers through inexpensive on-line tools. While these do-it-yourself versions are functionally viable, delivery through these platforms sends a subliminal message that says "Don't take this survey seriously, because we don't." The indirect message is often, "We will let you know if we receive good scores. Otherwise, we will never do anything with the information. That's why we didn't spend very much money on this." Home-grown isn't good enough for your business. You want solid satisfaction survey results that are achieved through a deliberate, sequential approach, and that you can act on. A measurement process is a fundamental tool for improving your organization's performance in the 1D territory.

Does your measurement system provide the information you need to manage your customer connections strategically? When you take the time and make the effort to measure customer satisfaction effectively, you communicate that your organization is willing to listen to customers and cares about what they say.

Customer loyalty is often touted as being much more important than customer satisfaction. Those who say this neglect to tell companies that loyalty requires an extensive knowledge of customer needs and what satisfies them. Customer satisfaction is the foundation of every successful company. You can't skip the satisfaction step and move straight into loyalty. An ongoing satisfaction measure will provide a realistic perspective of your organization's performance in the eyes of your customers.

Well-designed, actionable satisfaction measurements provide a valuable look at your operational quality and they will help your organization flex its muscle as a great supplier at the transactional level. They show your customers that you are developing your continuous improvement process by listening to and thinking like them. Taking action sends an uncompromising message to both customers and employees that customers matter and should be given as much attention as finance and operations.

Goal Setting
Once the basic customer satisfaction measure is in place, organizations have an ongoing gauge of the quality of their

performance up to the break-even point (Figure 4.1). It's now time to measure more than that. Today, the greater opportunity lies in measuring and leading the organization's dynamic journey into Customer 3D. This new perspective will measure how extraordinary the organization is in connecting with its customers. It will quantify the actions beyond the break-even point and will help everyone visualize the organization as a 3D entity.

It starts with goals. Every successful organization needs specific customer-centered goals. These go far beyond thinking of customers in terms of sales revenue and internal metrics related to how well you handle their problems. They also go beyond ongoing customer satisfaction goals for quality and performance improvements. Customer-centered goals tell employees where the business is heading. Developing these goals will require a dialogue among the goal-setting team members so there's a clear definition of what is considered "value" versus "non-value" in terms of the customer.

The process includes:

- Establishing a goal for the number of innovative ideas that are generated and a separate goal for the number of those ideas that get implemented. This involves tracking ideas submitted, creating a selection process, and logging those that are implemented.

- Determining how many processes and customer touch-points should receive a thorough evaluation. Assess what happened during the previous 12 months to determine a feasible goal for the next 12 months.

- Developing management education programs and creative events for customers to raise awareness in employees and to facilitate thinking like a customer. How many are needed? It depends on the size and structure of your organization.

Customer-centered thinking balances traditional business analytics with relevance for your customers. Being customer-centered makes your organization smarter and better able to execute its vision and purpose. It broadens your focus by challenging how changes will benefit the customer. But it won't happen without measurable goals.   173

Parametric Modeling. In the process of developing manufactured products – 3D modeling software is used to create the components that make up that product. Think of a manufacturer's parts manuals in which a subassembly might have 50 individual components. When one of these components changes, the other 49 parts change, accordingly. All of the information and spacial geometry for the product is linked so that when there are any changes to that computer model – all of the other components of the product automatically update. This is referred to as parametric modeling. Some changes are minor, such as a color change, and have little impact on related components. Other changes, such as size, have major implications. More material may be required, packaging changes, and shipping weights are influenced to name a few.

The business analogy equates to alignment and coordination between functional areas – the direct opposite of a "silo" mentality and the feeling that departments can operate independently.

Identify one process in your organization that is interconnected throughout the company. Brainstorm how, if this process were changed by one department and not communicated to other departments in your organization, would directly impact your customers. Continue to discuss strategies for bringing this (and other) processes in stronger alignment by defining the customer impact of changes before they occur.

Measuring the 3D Culture

Customer-centricity happens because a system is in place. You want to track how that system is performing. Measuring 3D performance requires calculating a Customer 3D Index for the overall organization and for any relevant departments or satellite locations. A Customer 3D Index provides a tangible measure for making an organization's customer strategy visible, which can be tracked over time, along with comparable measures of product and service performance across the entire organization. While the basic satisfaction index discussed earlier is reactive, the Customer 3D Index is proactive. While the traditional voice-of-the-customer metric is situational, the Customer

3D Index is organizational. The Customer 3D Index outcomes are focused on proactive/design thinking and drivers of positive outcomes for customers rather than traditional (reactive) problem-handling.

Customer 3D involves customer-centered ideas that are aligned across functions, and a customer-focused culture. It works because you are measuring your readiness to build stronger customer relationships. The Customer 3D Index is an ongoing evaluation of this performance, built around three internal metrics comprised of subcomponents, all measured for the overall organization and by department.

The Customer 3D Index indicates adherence to the organization's customer strategy. It's a dynamic gauge of how the customer-centered culture is evolving. After training employees in the new 3D approach, companies can use the Customer 3D Index to measure the progress of the organization. Knowing what you should be measuring – proactive ideas for customers, reduction in silo behaviors within the organization, and culture adoption – is fundamental. It goes beyond traditional 1D voice-of-the-customer and satisfaction measures to encourage empowerment and design thinking that solidifies readiness for customer-centered growth. It helps to understand the Customer 3D Index components:

▶INNOVATION
(Innovative approaches that will matter to customers)
The first component of a 3D approach is the capability for generating new ideas. This ability doesn't depend on voice-of-the-customer assessments, although customer feedback might be the catalyst. These are proactive ideas designed to improve service to the customer. Ideas are identified by metrics linked to monitoring value-added activities for the customer.

Proactive ideas that are well-communicated and implemented lead to innovative outcomes. The Customer 3D system is the most effective system for initiating and developing new ideas designed to benefit customers. The Customer 3D Index tracks the frequency of these ideas, and, in order to ensure that employees' ideas are properly

175

evaluated, it requires a process that clearly explains why ideas are rejected. Otherwise, employees will be reluctant to present new ideas in the future. Individual subcategories of the Innovation component include:

- The number of new product ideas generated (that add value to customers)
- The number of new product ideas implemented (and clear reasons why ideas aren't pursued)
- The number of new process ideas generated versus accepting status quo
- The number of new process ideas implemented (and clear reasons why ideas aren't pursued) versus accepting status quo

▶PERMEABILITY
(A measure of integration with the organization – silo-busting)

Undoubtedly, one of the greatest impediments to becoming a customer-centered culture is compartmentalization. The Customer 3D business strategy generates power through a comprehensive system that permeates the silos that exist in most businesses.

Since Customer 3D is a system of co-creation, it is critical to have all functional areas working together to find and improve processes for the customer's benefit. When these improved elements are in place, the organization passionately goes after those internal points that create waiting times and unnecessarily hard-to-explain procedures. Monitoring efforts in these areas provides a great barometer of the collaboration level while offering a measure of the organization's internal integration. It also keeps employee emphasis on questioning how the customer sees every process and how the company can improve it.

Therefore, the second component of the Customer 3D Index measures the collaborative level of internal processes. This is a metric for the silo-busting aggressiveness in your organization. The components of the permeability measure in the Customer 3D Index are:

- The number of cross-functional decisions on behalf of customers (not top-down decisions)

176

- The number of reviews of internal processes from the customer's perspective (searching for new process ideas)

The secret to facilitating smooth hand-offs in 3D organizations is empowering employees to make and distribute decisions about customers rather than forcing them to rely on top-down decisions. The metrics for these hand-offs to internal customers within the organization, often referred to as "next operation as customer" (NOAC) in quality terms, create measures for the smoothness of customer transactions. Rather than measuring inattention to quality, however, the Customer 3D Index measures the positive factors that drive these customer-centered outcomes in the internal culture.

In terms of permeability, Rochester, N.Y.'s The Strong is an organization without boundaries – making it highly permeable. Anyone, from any internal working team, may share their suggestions and generate ideas for solving problems. As an example, when the museum adopted its "Guest Services First" model, Kathie Dengler, senior vice president for guest and institutional services, set an expectation that members from every team across the museum – whether guest services, curatorial, security, or any other area – must adopt a guest-centric attitude. She said the needs of museum guests had to take the highest priority and that her own team would work closely with anyone who was reluctant to change how they were doing things – because change was mandatory.

Similarly, at financial advisory firm Veritat Advisors, the development group meets weekly to review feedback from recent client sessions, using the input to design process improvements. For example, the employees of the firm were able to identify a graph in a client report that didn't do what they needed it to – which meant that advisors spent too much time explaining the information contained in the graph. They changed it.

▶CULTURE AND PURPOSE
(Beyond product focus)

Underlying both the innovation and the permeability categories is the organization's culture and a measure of how well it fulfills its purpose. 3D organizations find a new purpose in delivering outcomes to customers that they value. Creating an environment

177

that deliberately reinforces this idea of individual and organizational achievement is critical. It leads a culture of innovation and entrepreneurship among employees.

The third measurement of Customer 3D, then, addresses how well the organization's leaders and employees are sustaining the positive 3D atmosphere and environment. Its measures of success draw on the number of:

- Fun, creative events generated for customers, such as clever ways to show off new services and ideas, placing customer videos on websites, sharing customer-submitted ideas or interesting ideas for using products, and holiday-related ideas that customers can enjoy
- Incidents of storytelling and public praise for customer-centered activities
- Training and brainstorming sessions about the organization's value to customers, including sessions on how to make values-driven decisions instead of relying on a rules-driven default

Storytelling and praise work on the principle of recurrence. When customer-centered actions are reinforced, they will happen again and again. Lots of communication will help employees understand the 3D organization's greater vision and work to support it instead of just working to sell. 3D employees believe in the company's purpose and they think their company's products are the best. They are generous and abundant in their customer interactions. And, they embrace community good will and partnerships rather than operating only in the company's self-interest.

Customer Perception

There's one more measurement factor which will complement the Customer 3D Index magnificently. Measuring external customer perceptions of whether your employees behave in a customer-centered way is important, so the final subcategory of the Culture and Purpose category of the Customer 3D Index is:

- Perception scores of external customers about how customer-centered the organization is and how well it adds value to their relationships

178

There must be a line of sight between your 3D performance and the perception of your customers. After all, the business wants the value that it is adding to be recognized. In your external voice-of-the-customer surveys and other feedback assessment tools, ask customers how pro-active they believe your organization is in developing ideas focused on customers. Ask them to score their perception on a 10-point scale and then transfer the average score to the index. Closely monitor the perceptions of customers to determine if your efforts are making a difference with them. If you're generating ideas, you want to make sure they're being noticed. This makes a nice reality check that will add deeper meaning to the Customer 3D Index.

How the Customer 3D Index Works

Customer 3D Index goals establish the direction that defines what customer-centering really means to the business. If your organization is only tracking these categories of 3D behavior informally, this index will make you better. They clarify what every employee should be trying to achieve, preventing misinterpretation. To make every aspect of these measurements quantifiable, it's important to attach specific metrics that you will monitor. The Customer 3D Index evaluates the success in three key elements of customer-centricity: innovation, silo-busting and culture.

The detailed measures are shown in Figure 7.1. The scoring is divided into three criteria, which reflect the customer strategy described in Chapter 5. The index is a measure of the organization's direction – not a basis for micro-managing individuals or departments. The following total points are possible for each category:

- 40 points for innovation
- 20 points for permeability
- 40 points for culture

CCI		Goal	Actual	% of Goal	Score
Innovation	New product ideas generated	10	4	40%	4.0
	New product ideas implemented	3	1	33%	3.3
	New process ideas generated	10	6	60%	6.0
	New process ideas implemented	5	2	40%	4.0
Permeability	Reviews of internal processes	4	2	50%	5.0
	Cross-functional process decisions	15	7	47%	4.7
Culture	Number of fun, creative ideas	10	8	80%	8.0
	Number of incidents of storytelling and praise	18	14	78%	7.8
	Training and brainstorming sessions	8	4	50%	5.0
	Customer perception of proactivity in the organization	10	8.5	85%	8.5
Total					**56.3**

Figure 7.1

The process begins when you assess your performance in these ten subcategories within the three key categories during the previous 12 months to get a baseline level. With the baseline done, you'll know where you need to put most of your efforts. The process of evaluating past performance will help establish specific goals in each of the ten subcategories. Set these goals based on what's realistic for your organization. A company with 100 employees, for example, might target one new idea per month, whereas a corporation with 10,000 employees would expect many more ideas. This is why the baseline is so important – it gives you a starting point.

The Customer 3D Index ultimately measures your alignment with customer needs along with how well the organization collaborates internally to meet those needs. It's a system for formalizing the future based on possibilities, rather than a future revolving around merely reacting to problems. It provides a structure for teaching employees how to understand and embrace customer-centricity, which in turn invites better comprehension of the organization's new direction. And, it fills that journey with contagious enthusiasm.

The Customer 3D Index focuses the organization on the key drivers of customer-centricity, which develops the trust of its customers in its higher performance capabilities. Without customer-centered goals, there's no way of knowing if progress has been made. The Customer 3D Index aligns each of the organization's departments using the metrics behind customer-centricity. Then, it distributes this mindset throughout the company so that everyone experiences the success and progress as a whole. It helps employees stay calm in the midst of activity and remain fully present for the customer. The cumulative effect is amazing. When an organization can look back over several months and identify the totality of the combined effort, everyone in the organization will appreciate the power of customer-centricity and its importance to the company's progress.

Reporting Results

Figure 7.2 illustrates an effective visual way to report the Customer 3D Index and the performance results in each subcategory. It lets the organization see the degrees of success and the gaps between the goals that were set. It also can be convenient for showing relatively short time periods, such as quarters, with cumulative information. The Customer 3D Index also allows organizations to monitor the speed with which the company improves, innovates, and invents.

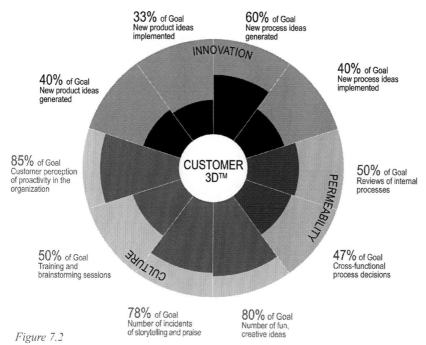

CUSTOMER 3D™ INDEX

33% of Goal
New product ideas implemented

60% of Goal
New process ideas generated

INNOVATION

40% of Goal
New process ideas implemented

40% of Goal
New product ideas generated

85% of Goal
Customer perception of proactivity in the organization

CUSTOMER 3D™

PERMEABILITY

50% of Goal
Reviews of internal processes

50% of Goal
Training and brainstorming sessions

CULTURE

47% of Goal
Cross-functional process decisions

78% of Goal
Number of incidents of storytelling and praise

80% of Goal
Number of fun, creative ideas

Figure 7.2

The percentages represent success of the organization against its goal in each component.

The Customer 3D Index is represented as a wheel to indicate the continuous nature of the process and the equality of each component. Customer-centricity will become more consistent when analytical techniques quantify the organization's quality of implementation. It forms the heart of the strategic diagnosis of the success.

Total System Benefits – It Becomes Easier to Manage

Successful 3D organizations have indicators and measures in place that tell them they are succeeding. The Customer 3D Index is an internal measure of how customer-centered the organization really is, with an external wedge that ensures customers are noticing the changes. It measures the fullness of the 3D culture.

The irony, of course, is that as the scores of the Customer 3D Index increase, the basic satisfaction index which measures the organization's 1D transactional performance also increases, perhaps due to a halo effect. Because they recognize the proactive value your organization is delivering, customers inevitably have higher regard for the organization's performance as they experience it through conventional touch points. For example, because the cultures at companies such as Barlean's Organic Oil, The Strong, cSubs and the others in this book are so outstanding at the 3D proactive performance level, tasks seem effortless at the 1D transactional level. Once any organization reaches the 3D level, it almost never has to worry about the teamwork required to carry out basic, everyday transactions. The beauty of this organic, purposeful behavior is that it becomes much easier to manage.

Customer 3D helps organizations become irreplaceable. Organizations that are truly customer-centered believe that maximizing customer value is their objective. When customers say to themselves, "I wish my supplier would…," it means there are still new ideas waiting to be developed. Proactive organizations never stop looking for these opportunities. They use the customer to tell the story of their future while using the Customer 3D Index technique to continue to grow into a provider of the highest value to customers.

The Customer 3D Index quantifies an organization's performance in the elements that matter in creating a 3D culture. It is the mathematics of a customer-centered organization. It is an assessment of the new customer basics for designing the future of customer relations, complementing the traditional indicators of satisfaction and loyalty. The Customer 3D system creates the framework that challenges organizations to renew their efforts every day to improve their performances for the customer. It puts demands (in a good way) on the imagination of employees for ideas of how to get better in the eyes of the customer.

3D Achievement

The Customer 3D Index demonstrates that Customer 3D success is not only possible, but can be duplicated or expanded. It creates patterns that help organizations become purposeful and strategic as they move toward their vision of customer-centricity. They are embracing ambitious, meaningful, and motivating goals while creating a sense of urgency. However, they must also embrace the persistence required to make the strategies successful. The Customer 3D Index provides everyone with self-awareness and ownership.

There is a sense of mission. Everyone shares a common view of the future and wants to contribute to getting there. This is far different from giving every employee the opportunity to please the customer and expecting them to take it. Redefine your customer mission, and the entire organization pursues the same comprehensive set of strategies. Align around the mission and commit to transparency.

There is an added benefit of the Customer 3D Index. It shows individuals across the organization how their work fits in the bigger picture. There is energy, because there's a point to what's going on. Everything ties together with a sense that everyone is moving in the same direction. The celebrations along the way explain where the organization is in its journey.

Employees begin to redefine their role from a functional "doer" to a caretaker, a leader, a consultant to customers. 3D organizations quickly notice that the Customer 3D Index does not dictate the inputs to the customer-centric journey – only the outputs, and that the employees have a great deal of freedom to accomplish them.

3D employees love the freedom it provides. There is still accountability, but it makes more sense to them. As a result, they

183

are willing to work hard because they know they have freedom to bring great ideas to their customers. The Customer 3D Index shows employees exactly where they are in relation to their goals and empowers them to track and manage their own progress. It fosters a sense of "whatever it takes" within the company. That attitude quickly removes obstacles.

Even Higher Goals

Measurement leads to even more ambitious goal setting, a crucial element of transformative leadership. Once the 3D culture is in place and initial goals are being achieved, organizations begin to believe in bigger, world-class goals. They are on a mission to change the trajectory of the organization's customer performance. They aren't just better than their competition; they are ready to make history. Organizations will elevate their thinking from "let's be more customer-centric" to "we want to be the most customer-centric company in our industry (or in the world)." Invested teams will want to set the bar higher.

Still, the larger your organization gets, the more challenging it is to manage tightly. The visibility of the Customer 3D Index helps with that by investing employees in the idea that this new focus on customer success will make a difference in their lives and the company's culture. The core of the solution is leadership – transformational leadership. Customer 3D strategies will help your organization build a system that supports the customer-centered outcomes that the company wants to accomplish. The Customer 3D Index will measure how well your performance is centered on those outcomes. Today's successful businesses are looking for opportunities to push the boundaries for their customers. This push needs a trained eye; the Customer 3D Index provides the navigation system for that eye, focusing on important information about the components that will drive that momentum.

A 3D organizational culture is built, not discovered. That is why the Customer 3D Index is the cornerstone of this building process. Reinforcement is a powerful force. Meaningful 3D performance data is critical to sustaining the journey. It helps to identify organizational obstacles that are getting in the way and to eliminate them. The index also help employees understand the impact they are having in helping the organization to add value to its customers.

EIGHT

Evidence

Don't bother just to be better than your contemporaries
or predecessors. Try to be better than yourself.
William Faulkner

Decades ago, people thought that nobody could run a mile in under
four minutes – until Roger Bannister did the "impossible" in 1954
and broke the four-minute-mile barrier with a time of 3 minutes
and 59.4 seconds. Becoming Customer 3D is a lot like being Roger
Bannister. 3D companies know "it" can be done, and they set out
to prove it. And just as other runners quickly set more records after
Bannister accomplished the "impossible," businesses that enjoy
initial 3D success begin enjoying even more success as employees
begin to see what's possible.

Customer 3D is a divergent system, leading to business growth
and possibilities for expanding in new directions that will create
higher value for customers and the company. Customers see 3D
organizations as the best in the field. The relationships developed
among Customer 3D operations become irreplaceable; as a result,
customers become unwilling to leave.

The effect inside the organization is equally powerful. It works like
compound interest, with gains folded back into the organizational
culture to produce even greater progress. Because it's grown

187

from a customer-centered purpose, the expansion into 3D gives organizations a stronger identity, top to bottom. All employees truly understand how they and their employer make a difference for others.

Customer-Centricity = Freedom and Loyalty

Becoming customer-centric is the best way to supercharge your organization. There are many advantages to this approach, but first and foremost are the increased profits that come with this business philosophy. Traditionally, companies that consistently meet customer product needs produce positive bottom-line results. In today's environment, where product attributes can be readily copied, this 1D performance isn't enough. Smart companies seek Customer 3D systems that will deliver higher returns by helping them become authentic champions of customer closeness. This is how they increase market share and the lifetime value of their customers.

Customer-centricity is a direction, not a place. Most organizations start their journey to increase customer relevance because of the financial benefits. There are many other reasons, of course, to become 3D, but let's focus on two critical elements that really define the impact inside the organization: organizational freedom and employee loyalty.

Customer-centricity produces freedom that manifests itself as employee empowerment. Because employees in 3D businesses have permission to customize or personalize how they treat customers, they don't have to deliver the lackluster, indifferent performances that tend to be the hallmark of 1D organizations. The freedom they enjoy rises out of confidence that everyone understands why they're working and whom they work for. Freedom also comes into play when a company works proactively on customer solutions, rather than reactively handling complaints and resolving customer issues. All of this translates to fewer worries and new opportunities for achieving greater heights. It facilitates a more decentralized organization that requires less top leadership approval of small decisions than in tightly controlled 1D models.

Companies also enjoy better employee loyalty when they embrace strong customer relationship values. While employees certainly want

188

to receive a paycheck, they care more about their customers than they do about the organization. I'm sorry to break that news to you, but research shows that employees get much of their job satisfaction from being able to deliver strong, common-sense solutions to customers. When employees are required to treat customers in ways they wouldn't want to be treated, they're less committed to their employers. Employees who are empowered to take care of their customers in ways that they like also like their jobs more – not a bad deal, is it? Customer 3D companies enjoy happier, more passionate employees and more committed customers.

Customer-centricity has another benefit: You never have to fight fires! How much time and how many resources are involved in solving problems created by 1D situations? Customer 3D organizations have been able to transcend these typical 1D events – including customer complaints, the need to re-do sub-par work, and general customer demands – to bring them to break-even status (see Figure 4.1). Customer 3D organizations have moved beyond all of this. The performance of 3D organizations on 1D transactions is so well addressed that these problems rarely happen. Issues with policies and procedures almost never occur because the organization is flexible and employees are empowered by the culture to do what's best for the customer and the relationship.

Hold On to Your Assets

With content and satisfied employees in place, you can focus on what you need to do to keep your current customers. In these challenging economic times, the competition is getting fiercer. Don't make the mistake of believing that repeat business is the same as customer loyalty. Complacency is dangerous. Counter it by taking custody of your customers and finding a strategy to not only keep them, but to dazzle them, too. This will get you the loyalty you need (and deserve). What worked a few years ago should be revisited and enhanced, because as is, those ideas probably aren't good enough to carry your company forward.

This churning of customers among 1D companies will become more prevalent, especially in uncertain economic periods when the maneuvering of market competitors will only become more calculated. Companies that ignore their customers will even allow

189

new competitors to emerge that are more customer-focused. "Business as usual" will quickly translate into falling behind. Unless your organization has a strong relationship and brand and, at the same time, anticipates your customers' future needs, it could experience a slide toward extinction. We all live on borrowed time with our customers, but, with the Customer 3D systematic effort, we can keep them longer.

Right now, your competitors are saying, "I can out-think you. I will lure your customers away by offering them innovative products and services that are easier, faster, and smarter and that provide them with solutions that they value. And, when I take your customer, I won't even ask for your permission." That's why merely hoping for continued success won't work anymore. Keeping customers is a full-contact sport and your game plan needs to be aggressive and proactive. Forward thinking involves anticipating a different future, with customers comparing your performance with ever-changing opportunities in the market. Staying ahead of your competition only happens when you and your team are thinking like your customers.

The Meaning of Loyalty

As you've discovered, thinking like your customer generates customer loyalty. Interestingly, the customer loyalty principles that have been promulgated for the last 20 years have all been presented from a "selling" viewpoint, concentrating on the advantages for the supplier's business in terms of customer retention, recommendation, and the efficiencies that come along with both. Of course it's always cheaper and more effective to keep a customer than to find a new one. But the nature of loyalty has changed.

While the word "loyalty" dates back to feudal times, the *Oxford Dictionary* defines it as "True or faithful (to duty, love or obligation); steadfast in allegiance, devoted to the legitimate sovereign or government of one's country." On that basis, why should anybody be loyal to any business organization? What legitimacy does the enterprise possess? Why do its customers have any duty to show allegiance to it? Of course they don't, and the more education, confidence and power consumers have, the more they realize it. In fact, in the 21st Century, it's the other way round. It's the customer who is king and the supplier who needs to be loyal to customers!

190

Because so many organizations accept that keeping existing customers costs less and is much more profitable than trying to win new ones, customer retention has become a major goal for businesses. Many companies are using customer loyalty to spearhead their retention campaigns, but I doubt that the loyalty concept is fully understood or effectively implemented by many of those embracing it. These organizations won't retain their existing customers without first adopting a philosophy that supports customer commitment.

Figure 8.1

In a 21st Century context, the translation of the Chinese version of the word for loyalty may lead us to an interpretation that is more appropriate for product and service providers than the feudal European version. During the 12th Century, Yue Fei of the Song Dynasty led an extremely disciplined army that would do anything for him. He had a tattoo of the Chinese character representing loyalty, shown here, on his back, and was fiercely loyal to his king. In the end, this led him to sacrifice himself for his country. The character literally means, as Yue Fei demonstrated, "from the center of the heart." That accentuates a more emotional side of loyalty and it is a more fitting way to describe the relationship with your leaders. It embodies a sense of purpose.

In today's business environment, organizations must deliver a meaning that captures the heart and soul of their customers. Loyalty has to be driven by a deep connection between customers and their suppliers – not some feudalistic allegiance or obligation that is founded on inequality between organizations and their buyers. The serious misunderstanding of this concept among managers and senior executives has been responsible for many misguided strategies devised in the name of securing customer loyalty. Whether you are the leader of a country or a company, loyalty has to be earned. How will organizations continue to attract increasingly educated and confident customers and keep them committed? The answer is simple: by listening, anticipating, and thinking like a customer. When organizations embrace the need to connect with their customers and lock in their hearts and emotions to their brand, then they understand the true meaning of loyalty.

191

Customer-Centricity is Worth It

Customer loyalty is one of the biggest reasons to switch to the customer-centric model, but it's not difficult to imagine the arguments against a change that's so profound: "Customer-centricity is an abstract idea. It involves a culture change. We prefer pragmatic results to ideology. Show us the benefits."

Much has been written about the "how" of customer-centricity, but not a lot about the "why." There's proof, of course, of the advantages. For example, in one study,[1] organizations with strong customer-centric cultures grew revenues by 682 percent during an 11-year period compared with 166 percent by their competitors. But it's easy to look at the evidence and declare that it doesn't apply to your company. Where's the tangible proof?

> Never interrupt someone doing what you said couldn't be done.
> *Amelia Earhart*

Remember the "Fosbury flop?" Dick Fosbury shocked the world at the 1968 Olympics in Mexico City when he broke the world record for the high jump – and captured the gold medal – by jumping over the bar backwards, face up, instead of frontwards, facing down. Today, virtually all Olympic-caliber high jumpers use the Fosbury technique. Customer-centricity is as transformative to a company's success as Fosbury's game-changing technique was to the high jump competition. Becoming customer-centered provides purpose to the corporate mission. It makes a difference because it is a unifying force for entire organizations. It will bring about cross-pollination of perspectives among departments, resulting in teamwork built around integrated mindsets, rather than segregated, silo mentalities.

Becoming the best must be a fundamental goal for leaders of customer-centric organizations. And, they must realize that they won't get there via the traditional product-centered path from the past. Their attitude has to be, "Either we become world-class or we leave the business," as Yogesh Chander Deveshwar, chairman and CEO of ITC Limited, expresses it in the book, *1,000 CEOs*.[2] 3D companies transform themselves by focusing on a corporate strategy that creates shareholder value while meeting the goals of customers and society. The proactive pursuit of excellence and sustainability for the customer is the kind of vision that structures all customer-centric organizations.

3D

Uncopyable. The hologram has developed into a low-cost security device for documents such as credit cards and currency. 3D thinking within organizations also makes them very difficult to copy.

List five process changes that could differentiate your organization from the competitors in your market and make your company harder to copy.

Figure 8.2
Photo credit: MasterCard

3D Leads to 3Cs – Starting with Customer Closeness

Becoming customer-centric is a choice. What is the payback for this choice? Developing a 3D organization leads to 3Cs – customer closeness, competitive advantage, and customer certainty.

Customer closeness is the secret weapon that high-performing organizations use to minimize risk in their businesses. We can distill that approach down to two key techniques that great 3D companies employ. First, these companies are, to borrow Peter Drucker's term, "monomaniacs with a mission." They are obsessed with focusing their resources on their customers. Direct customer relationships are critical success factors, so the percentage of employees from 3D companies in regular contact with customers is higher than in 1D operations. Because they are closer to the customer than their competitors, they are poised for quick reactions to changes in customer needs or new technologies. They are passionate and purposeful about maintaining communications with customers so that problems are minimized.

Second, 3D champions collaborate extremely well on innovations for customers. They operate in narrow target markets instead of chasing diversification; they work fanatically on serving the customer needs in those markets. They avoid the risk of distraction from their core

193

business by connecting with customers to develop improvements. The focus on meeting customer needs fosters growth which, in turn, has made these 3D companies the best performers in their industry. They have, through customer closeness, created a culture of proactive customer-centered ideas.

When your customers send their other vendors to you to figure out what to do, you know you're close to your customer. Subscription management company cSubs had a chance to enjoy how that felt when a major client brought all of its large vendors into a new platform for electronic invoicing. While most of the other companies had technical problems with the new system, the cSubs transition went so smoothly that the client asked the company to help its other vendors. cSubs was more than willing to assist. That is the type of exceptional behavior that helped them to be selected for Inc. Magazine's "5000 Fastest-Growing Private Companies in America."

3D organizations are refreshing because in many ways they are so "normal" and unpretentious in their performance. But these companies are far from average. They operate their businesses with an "actions speak louder than words" mindset. These 3D superstars have been willing to do the work necessary to structure a business model that is advantageous to customers. Rather than operating in an environment of risk and uncertainty, they embrace customer needs to make their own organizations better.

Is there anything better than something that helps your customer and brings you more business at the same time? Probably not. The National Parks Service passport program is a great example of how to do this. Introduced in 1986, it creates customer closeness by functioning as a travelogue with maps and information that help focus your search for vacation or general travel destination information. Park visitors fill their parks passports with official park stamps and additional information about their visits. It becomes, in essence, a personal scrapbook that organizes every park visit into one concise reference.

The hidden advantage of this passport system is that it provides customers with knowledge of the National Parks Service facilities they might not have otherwise known about. Many companies struggle with the fact that customers who know and use them for one product or service pigeon-hole them without realizing what else the company has to offer. The passport offers up every location operated by the service in a creative and engaging way. Both you and the customer benefit when the customer visits your site (whether it's real or virtual) more often because you make it more interesting or valuable.

At Barlean's, they encourage closeness with a really simple internal system. Every customer has a personalized number. When I order from them, my customer number is SelfBi000 (4-digit last name, 2-digit first name and 3 numbers). When a company, such as Whole Foods, orders from them, the customer number is WholFo000, with each store within their corporation given a unique 3-digit number. This simple identification system allows every employee at Barlean's to easily recognize the customer on a personal level. It provides context and reminds them that they are dealing with an individual customer – not a number.

Operating at 3D not only improves connectivity with customers, it also strengthens core competencies. Becoming customer-centered means you've created a "system" for customer closeness. Understanding the criteria for the success of this system requires a culture that is genuine in its belief that it must think like a customer. It is fundamental, but powerful, and when implemented properly, it will raise awareness in employees that they are empowered to take your business to the next level on behalf of the customer. Success, however, only occurs through a concentrated effort.

The Second C – Competitive Advantage

To enjoy the next of the 3Cs in 3D, a competitive advantage, companies need to outperform all others. This level of performance occurs only when a company implements a structured system to proactively exceed customer expectations. Outperforming delivers higher value for your customers; it's the new way to differentiate organizations.

When Michael Porter published his landmark book *Competitive Advantage* in 1985, the techniques he described focused on product differentiation. He mentioned customers on just 12 of the 536 pages.

Today, that playing field has changed significantly. As noted earlier, it's getting difficult to differentiate your products for longer than six months because they can be easily copied. The new competitive advantage is in customer-centered performance as seen through the lens of the customer.

There's a Woody Allen short story[3] about invaders from outer space who were not light years ahead of us – they were just 15 minutes ahead of us. This "15-minute competitive advantage" is no longer too far from reality. Organizations now must sense, feel, think, and act in ways that relate to their customers to have a competitive advantage.

Years ago, the large corporation I worked for had a very demanding client. The customer service staff groaned every time he made a special request. In less than two years, however, we were implementing all of his special requests as the standard operating procedure for all customers. Just like the majority of companies at the time, we were carrying out procedures in a way that was convenient for us, rather than thinking about what was best for the customer. Success now depends on welcoming new ideas for adding value to your customers instead of fighting them – especially when the ideas come from customers.

Teach your organization to outperform. Challenge your staff to continuously innovate in ways that matter to your customers. Build a culture that measures progress and celebrates high praise from customers for great performances. Design a knowledge process that is unrestricted, empowering, comfortable with exploration, and accepting of customer-centered trial and error.

You can make money following the lead of others in the market, but that approach will not help you reach greatness. Outperforming in ways that provide a competitive advantage will form a new identity for your organization and become the heart and soul of its cultural change. Outperforming will create a brand that is unforgettable.

In contrast, it is always surprising when new businesses open without a unique value proposition for customers to set them apart. For example, there's a new car wash near my home, where there are already plenty of those types of businesses. I am curious what

196

the owner plans to offer customers to make the business stand out or how the owner will make employees feel like they are truly providing high value to all customers. Will they outperform for customers? I wonder if they believe the business can be successful without being unique.

When organizational cultures are driven by generous, abundant behavior, they create a pattern of expansive improvement. The resulting actions attract customers who observe a corporate behavior designed to improve their lives (not the suppliers' internal costs). It creates a sense of attachment that strengthens customer loyalty. Leaders of extraordinary companies believe in always giving more than they expect to receive.

The Strong museum works diligently to make sure that its customer service provides it with a competitive advantage in a city with many other museums. Kathie Dengler, senior vice president for guest and institutional services, is passionate about the advantage her staff's performance gives the museum. "It's not about what you do or what you sell. What you do differently will set you apart," she says. "We are competing with many other venues for our guests' discretionary money. Our differentiator is guest service and the implied promise that we will take care of their needs." Since The Strong changed to a family-friendly, customer-centered organization in 2004, annual attendance has increased 350 percent and membership has grown from 2,000 to 18,000 members.

Branding Your Competitive Advantage

When your competitive advantage is your ability to outperform, that becomes your brand. The old paradigm was to brand your product, then add customer-centered behavior as icing on the cake. That product-centric approach misses huge opportunities. If you have a highly differentiated culture that is empowered to provide customers with value, users will say, "I have discovered something remarkable and I want to tell you about it." Your customers become your spokespersons.

> It is the mark of a good action that it appears inevitable in retrospect.
>
> *Robert Louis Stevenson*

Give them plenty of reasons to talk about how customer-centered your entire organization is and how you make

197

products better by thinking like a customer. Bring your employees along with this movement, as well, by encouraging them to walk the talk on this new, different brand promise.

What companies have built their brand around being customer-centric? A few come to mind – Nordstrom, Zappos, Amazon, Ritz-Carlton – but not many. That's not to say that other companies don't provide good transactional service to their customers, because many do. But where's the buzz about them being customer-centered? The point is that these other companies are known for their products, while their reputation for customer relationships is seen as an "add-on."

What if, alternatively, you chose to brand your skill at outperforming for customers? You have developed your organization significantly beyond helping customers become satisfied with good transactional service to a point where it's driven by a culture of pro-activity and fresh ideas that create value. This differentiation can be branded. It's a promise to continue to outperform for those customers every time they do business with you. This new brand can be powerful. Very powerful. Customers know they will never be disappointed or betrayed. If it's part of your intrinsic value, communicate it.

One caution, however: Branding can't be done in name only. It has to be authentic and instilled in the heart and soul of your organization. It also has to register with customers – they have to notice it. But if you're committed to world-class customer performance, it will benefit you. Branding this customer-focused change in your culture makes good business sense; promoting it as your brand will show how serious you are about delivering it.

Set this goal for your organization: customers will refer to you as incredibly customer-centric. Then distinguish your business from the competition by turning that identity into your brand. Use your customer-centricity as you would anything of value to differentiate your brand.

Customers view 1D companies in terms of brand "sameness," so real growth is challenging for these businesses. 1D organizations work frantically to differentiate themselves from their competitors through minor changes that are barely noticed – if at all – by customers. In most cases, these one-dimensional businesses are reluctant to risk significant change. In the end, as they tweak and re-tweak small product features, they end up delivering the same product variations as their competitors. So where's the differentiation? They're trying to appear different – assuming different is better – without really changing much. Even though they know the world is changing faster than ever before, they still want to play it safe.

Companies should be asking: What can we give our customers that they need, and that would make us really different? Being customer-centered is the essence of differentiation. 3D organizations deliver the products that customers truly believe are better – and they are, because the products have been designed with customer needs in mind.

Those in the quality profession work with the "cost of quality" concept. Essentially, it measures the failure to deliver quality products and services. The lower the number, the better. The theory behind the cost of quality metric is if we spend more time preventing problems, we'll need to spend less time later dealing with them. If there's a "cost of quality," perhaps there should be a "cost of differentiation," too, to measure how different we are (or aren't). It would measure the impact of giving customers greater value than competitors do. Measuring differentiation would encourage more proactive ideas from the company to stay ahead of the curve. To put this in context, the cost of differentiation in the MP3 player category in pre-iPod days turned out to be millions of dollars.

Barlean's Organic Oils differentiates itself by focusing on doing what it can to offer customers a healthier lifestyle rather than by copying the competition. Whereas other companies in the industry send the 10 percent residue from the flax manufacturing process back through the process a second time, Barlean's believes that this diminishes the freshness and quality of the product for customers. That's why the company recycles its residue through local farmers, who use it as a feed supplement for cows. When suppliers embrace customers and their needs instead of watching what competitors are doing, the game changes. Not only does the customer benefit, but confidence in the company's ability to serve customer needs improves dramatically.

199

This leads to even more innovation. The paradox is that in order to be different from your competitors, you must ignore them. If you are constantly looking at what your competitors are doing, you will simply end up imitating each other.

The Third C – Customer Certainty

What's better than customer loyalty? Customer certainty, the third C in the three Cs of 3D. An organization that is certain it is focused on delivering the highest value for its customers is a confident organization. It knows that customers see it as distinctly better than others in the industry. When you're providing what customers need, you have customer certainty.

You have to pass through customer loyalty on the journey to customer certainty, though. If you want to be certain that your clients are going to return again and again and never leave, design a culture in which every touch point is evaluated from the customer perspective. It must be an environment that develops new ideas, big and small, that will create a place of distinction rather than sameness. This is what generates loyalty.

There is no complete certainty with customers, though. The best you can do is to distance your organization from uncertainty. You do that by being superior, and superiority comes from being customer-centered. Think about what matters most to your customers, rather than how to temporarily maneuver ahead of your competition.

Barlean's efforts have paid off with solid loyalty among its customers. One retailer said, "They knew people were looking for a more flavorful way to benefit from the nutrition value in fish oils. They created a palatable option, the Omega-3 Swirl beverages. This has helped generate a group of customers in our store who are now immensely loyal to Barlean's."

One of the company's competitors has a wider overall product selection than Barlean's does. However, Barlean's doesn't let that change their customer vision. "We want to get to the point where customers ask our competitors, 'Do you do it like Barlean's does it?'" says Scott North, director of customer services.

200   In other words, are you 3D yet?

Generating customer loyalty and the resulting customer certainty is hard work. It is even more difficult for a new, unproven company, because that business doesn't have a customer base. Every business must differentiate itself by providing more value to its customers. Being customer-centered brings better clarity to organizations because it focuses them on what's most important: thinking like a customer instead of a competitor.

Hyper-Loyal Customers Are the Best Customers

It's been argued that today's customers are less loyal than ever before. They expect more for their loyalty and tell fewer people about what you do right. If that's true, however, then why do some organizations have customers who are "off the charts" with their loyalty? Hyper-loyal customers are true fans that tell others about how much they love that company. 3D organizations have many, many hyper-loyal customers.

These people are passionate about converting others to become members of their "club" so that they can have the same great experiences. Stacy Perman talks about this in her book about fast-food hamburger chain, In-N-Out Burger. "Its loyal fan base… often did the heavy lifting, frequently boasting about their zealous affection for the chain to everybody else," she writes in *In-N-Out Burger*. "The chain's regulars assumed the responsibility of bringing in a constant stream of new devotees, an act generally referred to as 'the conversion.' It had the feel of bestowing membership into a club that seemed at once exclusive and egalitarian."[4]

Customers in a strong supplier relationship like this are happier when there are other customers doing business with you, too. It makes them feel smarter (because they found you) but at the same time, they want others to share the good experiences. This is when customer certainty kicks in – it happens when current customers feel compelled to convert others. This goes far beyond a traditional "willingness to recommend" question on a survey. At the opening of the first In-N-Out in Texas, for example, hyper-loyal customers slept overnight to stake their claims as the first in line and the first person at the drive-through window of the new location. Success means winning the hearts and minds of the market. If done right, it's contagious. People will have an unconditional love for your services because they trust that you are always designing new solutions for them. Hyper-loyalty is your goal when reframing the customer-centered efforts in your organization.

Being customer-centric means you are loyal to your customers, too. When customers realize this, they reciprocate. It's a symbiotic relationship. Customers become less loyal if you have lost touch with them, so Barlean's Organic Oils calls everyone who hasn't ordered in six weeks. Employees call this their "Missing in Action" program. It has resulted in a 95 percent customer retention rate in the past 10 years. But you also lose touch when you focus on things that don't matter to them. The antidote, of course, is connecting with their belief systems even more deeply. Being customer-centered means moving your culture to a whole new level – where people not only buy from you, but they love you and want you to continue to get better. They want to be around you because they know you are the best and will keep getting better. They're hyper-loyal.

While 1D organizations report that customers are less loyal than in the past, 3D organizations are using the loyalty of passionate customers to convert new customers. What have you done lately to convert your present customers to higher levels of loyalty?

Because 3D organizations have the 3Cs – closeness to the customer, competitive advantage, and customer certainty – they have customers who are eager to provide testimonials. These often unsolicited comments raving about products or services – or how customers are treated – can be used as part of the branding process to communicate clearly and effectively how your company differs from all others.

Beautiful Evidence
Business leaders want what Edward Tufte[5] calls "beautiful evidence" that their companies will become better and even unique when they become Customer 3D. And the evidence has to be motivating. Otherwise, the effort will become sidetracked because of scattered forces.

Keeping customers requires staying more closely in tune with their experiences than ever before. Customers want the best price from your organization, and thanks to the Internet, they can easily find out what your competitors charge. The barriers to leaving you for a lower-priced alternative are much lower. Although they might continue to buy from you, their comments to others about you might not always be accurate or positive. In addition, in most cases, your most loyal customers have higher expectations from your organization than your average customers. Customer-centricity has come of age primarily because the customer has many more options than in the past.

It is remarkable how many issues get resolved when Customer 3D becomes instinctive to an organization. Problems such as employee morale, inefficiencies due to handling customer complaints and employees asking managers for answers to routine questions from customers seem to disappear with a customer-centered purpose. Being product-centered is dispiriting to businesses and employees because it unrealistically expects customers to behave in traditional ways. Worse, when businesses are supplier-centered, it's much more difficult to detect "drift" in their customer focus. Ambiguity can and will set in.

Using the Customer-Centered Index ™ described in Chapter 7 is the key to making the connection. It puts the ambiguous into an ordered, recognizable and repeatable system. It's a measure of the quality of the interactions your organization has with your customers. It provides specific data that takes your organization's buy-in from "soft" benefits to a straightforward, tangible understanding of the behaviors that provide value for your customers. If you're transitioning to being more customer-focused, it's critical to define and measure the impact those changes will have.

In the journey toward becoming customer-centered, organizations must develop their own evidence, based on what they have determined to be most important in driving deeper customer value. Using the Customer 3D Index, they can track improvements against profits and customer satisfaction to clearly understand the influence that "thinking like a customer" has on their overall performance. Customer-centricity is transformative. Now, with a valid measurement system, its time has come.

For companies that want to become more customer-centered, the evidence of the solid benefits for the organization is undeniable. In addition, with the clear definition of the process that exceptional organizations have been using, the journey is now straightforward and more easily achievable. The following pages provide a short outline of the steps in the Customer 3D system.

HOW TO DEVELOP THE CUSTOMER 3D SYSTEM IN YOUR ORGANIZATION

The Customer 3D system begins with a customer-centered purpose and ends with results that the customer will value. This company-wide purpose is built up around a universal concept – **value for the customer**. The practical side of this purpose manifests itself not as transactional events that employees deliver, but as the many, many proactive ideas which employees deliver, which can be replicated throughout the organization and which will create performances for customers that exceed the competition.

If you follow these steps, you will successfully create and sustain a customer-centric culture throughout your organization.

▶ DESCRIBE ◀

Step 1: Create a customer-centered purpose. This provides meaning to the work each employee does. It is rewarding for employees.

Example, *[Our organization]'s purpose is _____ for the customer.*

Contrast this 3D purpose with a traditional 1D perspective, which might be: *[Our organization]'s purpose is to sell (our product or service).*

So, for example, a newspaper company narrowly could say, *"We are in the business of selling newspapers"* or at the 3D level it could think in terms of how they can benefit the customer. In that case, they could say, *"We are in the news and information business and our purpose is to keep our customers well-informed, regardless of the media that we use to deliver this information."*

A manufacturer of nutritional supplements broadly believes that its purpose is a healthier lifestyle for its customers, rather than simply to sell healthy supplements. Therefore, employees see their work and their value in not only having

205

customers buy products, but to provide information to as many consumers as possible so that they can benefit.

Reinforce what this purpose means. Introduce legacy storytelling about the history of the company and the core values that should drive behaviors toward customers. Showcase the founders' beliefs about customers and historical company events that illustrate value-added performances for customers.

Create a sound bite statement that summarizes and enhances your customer-centered purpose (See Chapter 5). This should present a broad outcome and drive a "no holds barred" approach that gives employees freedom to perform as long as they produce that outcome for customers.

▶ DEVELOP ◀

Step 2: Build up the proactive organizational culture, layer on layer, by educating employees about the customer-centered purpose. Set parameters for creative behaviors that will add value to customers. Regularly assess employees' perception about whether the company is doing meaningful work and whether they feel a part of the success. Teach **'transformative' not additive**. Teach **'abundance' and win-win instead of scarcity**.

Begin with a single project – the improvement of a process that will impact many customers. Once the demand is started based on a customer need and/or proactive solution, designate a champion or a team to carry it out. It has to be evaluated based on the investment and outcomes.

Consistently "call out" product-centric (1D) behaviors that employees encounter in other companies. Because employees don't like to receive that type of treatment, they should be empowered to eliminate it for their customers.
Make 3D the common language of the organization. Educate the culture about internal simplicity. Encourage the employees to look for and streamline internal processes and territorial actions that create complexity for the customer. **Teach collaboration.**

Step 3: Create a customer strategy that goes beyond the Voice-of-the-Customer survey component and basic performance quality measures, which should already be business-as-usual in every organization (even the 1D variety). This targeted customer strategy should focus only on the three elements of 3D success – **innovation, permeability** (silo-busting), and a **culture that is proactive for customers**.

Encourage a consultative approach to external actions, in which employees are the experts in helping customers to be more successful in their jobs and in their lives. The secret to make this consulting role work is to give the organization a challenge (to look for ways to find more value for customers) along with the freedom to allow employees to master the challenge. This new strategy should complement and share equal prominence with the organization's financial and product strategies which are already in place. Its reason for being is that it's the right thing to do; but it is grounded in the belief that it is also the best way to differentiate your company from its competition.

▶ DELIVER ◀

Step 4: Establish quantitative goals for each element of the customer strategy and convert these to an ongoing Customer 3D Index metric. Otherwise, execution might be uncertain.

Design thinking: Facilitate the **Discover-Design-Deliver** creative process by establishing a straightforward method for evaluating innovative customer-centered ideas. Define each idea by the value it brings to the customer. Ideas could be new or they could be process improvements. Put a dollar figure on the benefit to customers and the value added inside the organization through process savings.

Make TLC (Thinking Like a Customer) discussions a part of every meeting inside the company. Require every meeting agenda to include time for these discussions about how actions will create a more customer-centered organization. Design a system to capture new ideas that are developed and actions to be taken to execute them.

207

Praise customer-centric behaviors by employees through storytelling and frequent meetings in departments and company-wide. It reinforces that the new ideas are growing and that the organization is not standing still in its efforts for customers.

Ask employees and departments to share examples of the WE approach (actions based on *What Else?* the customer would value) with the rest of the organization through a clearinghouse function with the company. A dynamic knowledge sharing system is one of the keys to the company's success. It eliminates redundancy. The capability to generate and share this knowledge will be what differentiates the company. 3D organizations excel at making this knowledge visible. Share information and research gathered during answering customers' questions and consulting with them. The ideal solution would be to organize this information into a central location, which is accessible by all co-workers. You don't want to make employees reinvent the wheel. The more they know, the faster they can build on it.

Outcomes: The Customer 3D system is fundamental to achieving coherence. It brings together the diverse functions within any organization. If you want to be the most customer-centered organization in your market sector (or the world), Customer 3D is the system that will energize the customer-centered culture that will propel you to that new dimension.

NINE

A Stronger 3D Future

Don't stop, thinking about tomorrow,
Don't stop, it'll soon be here,
It'll be, better than before,
Yesterday's gone, yesterday's gone.
Christine McVie, Fleetwood Mac

The organizations cited as good customer-centric examples in this book have several traits in common. They:

- Are driven by a purpose, which is usually to be an industry change-maker for their customers
- Aren't afraid to push past the margins by anticipating customer needs
- Share a passion for delivering high quality to their customers
- Have made changes that are organizational rather than transactional
- Realize that the traditional, product-centric way is static and destined for sameness
- Place the customer at the center of their operation
- Are prepared to change in unison with the customer

These businesses are on a journey from the mechanistic, product-centered world to a more humanistic, stronger and customer-centered place. This transition is taking organizations and their customers on a trip that leads to a higher level of performance by allowing customer-centered ideas to develop and thrive.

209

3D organizations are well-positioned to avert disaster because they connect with their customers in a "dimension" that goes far beyond their products and services – this makes them less vulnerable to the ebb and flow of economies and industries. Customer 3D is the most effective business model for the future because its organic, authentic approach delivers a sense of possibility. As products become commodities and competition increases, customer-centering is the best way to differentiate your business from all others. But you must take action now, and make the process happen quickly. If you move too slowly, the Customer 3D system will never take hold in your organization.

Customer 3D organizations understand that customer-centered improvements are transformative, not just add-ons. These changes impact connections with customers and authenticate the three-dimensional culture within the organization. 1D businesses will look at many of the ideas from the high-performing companies in this book and think that they can be successful by simply adding one or two of them to their operation, but it doesn't work that way. A solid organizational future will rise from a foundation built around a well-understood strategy for what the business wants to accomplish for customers. Educated, Internet-savvy consumers will gravitate toward companies that offer a customer-centered persona that is evident in their products, their people, and their processes. This is the 3D image.

3D Benefits
3D companies outperform for their customers without increasing operating costs. How is this possible? They can accomplish this because the day-to-day activities of 1D companies become easier and more logical. Fewer rules are necessary; the cohesion between individuals and departments reduces mistakes and delays. Simply put, the culture manifests itself not only in closer connections with customers, but in an overall organization that looks better – *way better* – to the customer, too.

Long-term, the 3D system of customer-centering delivers:

- An organizational culture that provides customers with a higher value that is recognized and appreciated

- A motivated workforce focused on proactively taking care of customers with a consultative, positive attitude that takes the place of a product-selling approach
- A definitive style when working with customers that is unique to the organization

3D is stronger than 1D. It gives an organization strength and coherence. But it doesn't happen accidentally – it requires commitment, thought and training. The customer centering must be intentional; the focus needs to be on re-orienting the culture away from a product-based attitude. 3D is nothing short of a reinvention of the business – a necessary reinvention!

Customer 3D transforms corporate cultures by employing a simple system that produces better-than-today outcomes for customers. It creates the ability to see the thousands of customer touch points as opportunities. Becoming 3D enables organizations to recognize a different, more promising story for the business – one they haven't had the courage to imagine until now.

When companies embrace the 3D model, they enjoy a rebirth of spirit. Considerable power is unleashed with 3D customer connections, creating a more successful future for organizations. Most importantly, when companies replace their product- or supplier-centric mentality with one that is customer-centric, a new energy emerges in the organization. That new energy manifests itself in greater creativity, empowerment, and uniqueness that attract customers. And, best of all, it's sustainable because it enjoys built-in adaptability and responsiveness to customer needs.

Some 1D organizations believe they're customer-centered in spite of the fact that customers are unhappy because many of their needs aren't met. These businesses aren't fooling anyone but themselves, and, unfortunately, this stance isn't effective anymore. Successful companies need a dynamic, customer-centered strategy. Lubricant manufacturer WD-40, for example, values its fan club members and the feedback that they provide about usage and product ideas. The company also shares product tips and fun videos with members and allows them to ask questions and leave comments in a community forum.

211

Like WD-40, the Customer 3D organizations highlighted in this book are driven by the passion to create an outstanding experience for their fans. While they might not have a formal fan club, they behave as if they do. They know that their future success and growth will depend on their relationships with employees and customers – not on products that will eventually become obsolete, less expensive, or easier to copy.

The Quiet Revolution

Many well-intentioned companies announce to anyone who will listen that they want to exceed customer expectations. But we do business in a world with demanding consumers who have become accustomed to "unexpected" service at the transactional level – a coffee shop barista compensates for a long wait with a coupon for a free drink or a hospital employee walks a visitor to the destination instead of providing a string of directions. What was once unexpected has become de rigueur in the drive to differentiate one organization from the next.

> We shrink from change; yet is there anything that can come into being without it?
> *Marcus Aurelius*

The true advantages come from innovative organizational performance. There's a quiet revolution happening, one in which customer-focused companies are using new ideas to create unexpected and valuable experiences for all of their customers – not just a select few.

Mahatma Gandhi challenged us to "be the change you wish to see in the world." Progressive companies that are committed to transforming themselves into customer-centered entities are, indeed, trying to produce a positive, change-the-world outcome for customers. This re-orientation is happening because 3D businesses are changing their view of what is possible. They are moving forward by reinterpreting what they do and how they do it from the perspective of their customers. The trend is both logical and refreshing because it's based on the importance of proactively delivering what customers need and want before they ask for it.

3D Flexibility. When I.M. Pei designed the Bank of China building in Hong Kong, he used a three-dimensional frame instead of the conventional column-and-beam architectural approach that required heavy bracing with additional steel for the outside members to withstand typhoon winds. The extra bracing was required because traditional skyscrapers in Hong Kong were basically tall versions of smaller buildings designed on boxlike frames.

"Instead of relying on stiffening the two-dimensional sides of the standard box, Pei used a three-dimensional frame, or space truss, whose members penetrated through the building itself. These members united the vertical planes of the four faces of the building and allowed wind loads to be transferred to the four corners, which were steadied with reinforced columns. In addition to bracing against wind, the trusses supported most of the weight of the building. Since the structure itself had become the bracing, less steel was required, making the building relatively easy to build. This was not a simple Modernist case of form following function, but of both proceeding simultaneously."[1]

How would moving from a stiff product-centered structure to a more flexible customer-centered approach make the culture easier to "build"? How would this mentality make the organization more resilient to outside forces than it is today?

Figure 9.1
Photo courtesy of Ian Lambot,
Bank of China Tower

Companies are remaking themselves using Customer 3D, expecting themselves to be more creative at every customer touch point. This intuitive thinking – the understanding that they can always challenge the business to design a product or service so it's better for the customer – is helping organizations continue to grow. It is game-changing. Imagine how 3D technology in movie theater glasses and other devices changes our visual reality to make our experiences more exciting, more realistic, and more enjoyable – it does the same for organizations.

213

Companies must be empowered to align their work more precisely with customers. Successful organizations are developing systems that will create new, unexpected approaches for customers. But these unexpected innovations resonate as valuable because they are designed by a well-developed organizational culture geared toward thinking like a customer. It's okay to change your customers' expectations, as long as you take them higher. The Customer 3D way of thinking and managing equates to a quiet revolution that measures its success by its ever-improving performance for the customer.

Better Solutions

Most organizations are held back by traditional strategies that cause them to act in familiar, repetitive ways. The successful ones, however, have allowed the emerging importance of customers to overcome this inertia. Design principles will help all organizations to begin thinking like their customers when developing novel process improvements.

3D organizations allow employees to focus their actions so that customers become more prominent in all business decisions. They use Customer 3D thinking to reboot their systems with a stronger purpose. The goal is to re-evaluate everything they do and sell from the viewpoint of whether it connects with customer thinking and delivers the highest possible value to those customers.

There is, frankly, a refreshing humility behind this shift. 3D companies, many of which are already high-performing, aren't afraid to admit that they can get even better. Every customer encounter is seen as an opportunity to discover a fresh way to improve the customer experience. It's an attitude that fosters greater customer closeness simply by seeing the possibility of a better solution – and acting on it.

Roger Martin, dean of the Rotman School of Management at the University of Toronto, has called this type of thinking "the productive combination of analytical thinking and intuitive thinking." Solutions-based thinking is not superficial; it is purposeful. It follows rules and proven principles. It is relevant to business because it is driven by a set of skills that can be developed in any organization. It is the optimistic way of the future, focused on discovering and implementing new ideas for customers. In fact, the results of this thinking can only be successful when approached with a positive bias for customers.

Visionary organizations with eyes on the future are, indeed, questioning the status quo and designing solutions that will help produce more abundant situations for their customers. The Customer 3D system can be the catalyst that businesses use to stretch their thinking on behalf of customers. It can help them create and implement ideas that would not been thought of a few years ago.

Spreading the Word

3D companies want others to be just like them. They aren't anxious about being copied – their values are based on an attitude of abundance, so they want to share their customer-centered philosophy with everyone. They are open and willing to share their information in the belief that all parties will prosper.

Customer 3D organizations are generous. They want to share their ideas. Scott North, customer service director of Barlean's Organic Oils, expressed this attitude when he said, "As an organization, we are hungry to change the world and the health

> Life gives to the givers and takes from the takers; life has a perfect accounting system.
> *Roxanne Emmerich*

of the world. Every person in the company is asked to be part of the change and asked to grow personally." All of the 3D organizations mentioned in this book are driven by this hunger to change the world. They have done it well inside their organizations, but they are also eager to share their successes in ways that will help other companies.

Customer 3D is not only an extra dimension that can make product-centered companies improve exponentially, it's a new system for introducing a wholeness and life to business that has been missing for too long. It establishes a higher, more positive culture that all employees are proud to share with their customers. 3D performance is dramatically more than 1D performance with a few things "added." It is a new dimension, expanding from an understanding that grows from experiencing the thoughts and needs of others. It is

215

the future that will change the way companies sustain success.

Customer 3D is natural, not lifeless. It creates an energy that can't be depleted. It transforms cultures by encouraging them to grow with a purpose. As you set out to shift your organization to customer-centricity, don't think about holding onto the 1D status quo; imagine the possibilities in 3D when you are thinking like a customer.

What's Your Number?

Nothing is forever, including your product. When the rules change regarding customer relations, you need a new approach. So, will your organization continue its 1D thinking or transform itself into 3D? What's your number – 1D? 2D? 3D?

> Winners must learn to relish change with the same enthusiasm and energy that we have resisted it in the past.
>
> *Tom Peters*

The surest way to grow – and to sustain that growth – is by being customer-centered. The proactive culture which is required to take your organization to that new dimension will be the foundation of its future prosperity. Companies that transform themselves from product-centric to customer-centric are the organizations that will survive and thrive for years to come.

Designing the future starts at the top. 3D organizations take a developmental stance regarding their future. They take the straightforward position that in two years, they will be different from today. However, this change means they will have to un-learn their 1D behaviors. By focusing on how they can create a more vibrant culture for customers rather than focusing only on their products, they challenge themselves to continuously ask how they can become more customer-centered. That internal challenging, of course, is the basis of all improvements.

"The paradox in creating the future is that you cannot predict the future."[2] That might be true, but because Customer 3D companies are closer to their customers' way of thinking than their product-centered competitors, they are prepared for whatever might be around the corner. We know it is impossible to draw an accurate picture of the future. But we continue to offer our best guesses because we want to know what the "great unknown" might hold. While we might see the future as having limitless possibilities, there is pressure in the short

216

term to invent the future for our customers before the competition does.

Ask your organization this question: What could our competitors be developing for our customers right now that we don't currently offer? Allow futuristic thoughts that will challenge the business to defend why it hasn't implemented them already. Then, explore the possibilities for designing these solutions within your company.

Discuss the question in brainstorming sessions where you encourage participants to:

- Break the rules to uncover fresh ideas
- Account for worst case scenarios
- Evaluate risk-reward tradeoffs

If people are too close to their industry's status quo, during this exercise they should imagine being customers in a completely different field. If they work in manufacturing, for example, they usually have no problem articulating what they want from their mobile phone company in the future. This exercise, of course, helps them look at their own products and services from the customer's point of view.

Don't approach this brainstorming process casually. Use a disciplined approach. When our firm facilitates this creative thinking with groups, we ask them to challenge market sector assumptions. The significant impact of new technology must always be considered, too. Participants must also figure out how to reverse engineer their futuristic ideas so they can implement them before competitors do.

Our views of the future are most often shaped by our perspective about how changes can occur logically, based on current trends. The future is, in fact, a series of small steps that lead to bigger change. Change happens progressively over years but we must aggressively pursue it, since it can happen faster than we think. That's why we have to be the architects of the future and create change in small ways that will lead to larger trends. When North of Barlean's was asked to describe the customer connection with his organization in two years, he answered, "No change, just fine-tuning the focus."   217

The most important factor, however, will be how customers feel about the changes. The goal is to listen to these stakeholders and try to improve the way they experience the world. Scenario planning, which used to be a luxury, is now essential for all parts of every organization. The good news is that it's doable. It requires a comprehensive knowledge of how the company does business now as well as its unmet customer needs. Get everyone in your organization focused on a different kind of future. It will generate heightened energy and inspire teams to work collectively on actions that will get you where you need to go.

3D organizations are unique, like fingerprints. They have developed a clear, expansive definition of customer success and the organizational freedom to deliver that success. The Customer 3D system doesn't want companies necessarily to be like other great 3D organizations. Instead, it helps practitioners emphasize the ways in which they are like no one but themselves. That comes from using your ability to outperform as your differentiator.

The future will belong to 3D organizations that have the closest connections with their customers. Being unforgettable to your customers happens when you design solutions – both products and services – for every customer touch point. When you make a better future possible for customers, they will become amazingly committed to you. You will create a space in your client relationships that is full of possibilities and great expectations for what can happen. It will be way ahead of your competitors – all because you framed your opportunities by thinking like your customers. So, what's your number?

Characteristics that Give 3D Organizations Longevity

3D organizations have greater staying power than their competition because their customer closeness makes them more relevant to customers. 3D companies:

- Do the right thing for customers
- Establish 3D goals and measure performance in order to fine-tune the value they are adding beyond what the status quo is creating
- Create a compelling brand based on their customer-centricity, not their products or services
- Stay original by being driven by possibilities
- Willingly share their ideas if they will help other organizations to better serve their customers
- Outperform by generating happiness for customers and employees
- Are ready for the future, whatever it brings

About the Author

With more than 25 years of business leadership, Bill Self's market research experience has allowed him to study what the extraordinarily customer-centered companies do well to separate themselves from their competition. Today, he concentrates on helping companies learn how to transform their organizations into market leaders by focusing on the success of their customers.

Self has developed the unique Customer 3D Index, a dynamic system designed to enable product-centric organizations to become customer-centered champions. He is also the president of the North American division of The Leadership Factor, a global firm specializing in customer research and he is a member of the National Speakers Association.

Customer 3D delivers the cutting-edge strategy which is elevating companies to a degree of closeness with their customers that is changing the way organizations differentiate their brand and performance. Bill actively shares his ideas and techniques at the widely read blog, www.thinkinglikeacustomer.com.

Notes

Chapter 1

1. Alvin Toffler's *Future Shock* (New York, NY: Random House, 1970), pages 113, 135.

2. Julia Kirby and Thomas A. Stewart, "The Institutional Yes," *Harvard Business Review* (2007).

Chapter 2

1. Frank Lloyd Wright, *Frank Lloyd Wright: An Autobiography*, (Petaluma, CA: Pomegranate, 2005), page 168. Originally published in New York by Duell, Sloan and Pearce, 1943.

2. Frank Lloyd Wright, quoted by Satish Kumar and Freddie Whitefield in Visionaries: *The 20th Century's 100 Most Inspirational Leaders*, (White River Junction, VT: Chelsea Green Publishing, 2007).

3. Gordon R. Sullivan and Michael V. Harper, *Hope is Not a Method* (New York: Times Books, a division of Random House, 1996), page 34.

4. Mark Goulston, *Just Listen: Discover the Secret to Getting Through to Absolutely Anyone*, (New York, Amacon Books, 2010), pages 112-115.

5. Dev Patnaik with Peter Mortensen, *Wired to Care: How Companies Prosper When They Create Widespread Empathy* (Upper Saddle River, NJ: FT Press, 2009), pages 20-21.

6. Michael Jones, "The Roots of Aliveness – Leading as a Living Process", *The Berkana Institute* (copyright 2007, by Michael Jones), <http://www.berkana.org/articles/rootsofaliveness.html>.

7. Michael Jones, "The Roots of Aliveness – Leading as a Living Process", *The Berkana Institute* (copyright 2007, by Michael Jones), <http://www.berkana.org/articles/rootsofaliveness.html>.

8. From the major writings of Henri Matisse, quoted in Jack D. Flam, *Matisse on Art* (Berkley, CA: University of California Press, 1995).

9. Christopher Alexander, *The Nature of Order, Book One: The Phenomenon of Life*, (Berkeley, CA: The Center for Environmental Structure, 2002).

10. Peter Drucker, *The Practice of Management*, (New York: Harper Collins, 1954, renewed in 1982).

Chapter 3

1. Jim Collins, *Good to Great*™ Diagnostic Tool, page 5, developed by Jim Collins, 2006, in conjunction with his book, *Good to Great: Why Some Companies Make the Leap...and Others Don't*, (New York: Harper Business, 2001).

2. Ken Blanchard and Garry Ridge, *Helping People Win at Work*, (Upper Saddle River, NJ: FT Press, 2009).

3. Quoted by Henry Mintzberg in *Managing* (San Francisco, Berrett-Koehler Publishers, 2009), page 67.

4. Tony Hsieh, *Delivering Happiness - A Path To Profits, Passion, and Purpose*, (New York: Business Plus, 2010).

5.   Ori Brafman and Rom Brafman, *Click: The Magic of Instant Connections*, (New York: Broadway Books, 2010).

Chapter 4

1.   Shoshanah Cohen and Joseph Roussel, *Strategic Supply Chain Management*, (New York: McGraw-Hill, 2004).

2.   Edward de Bono, *Six Thinking Hats* (New York NY: Back Bay Books, 1999).

Chapter 5

1.   David Collis and Michael Rukstad, "Can You Say What Your Strategy Is?," *Harvard Business Review* (August, 2008), page 84.

2.   Collis and Rukstad, "Strategy," page 87.

3.   Steven Johnson, *Where Good Ideas Come From: The Natural History of Innovation*, (New York: Riverhead Books, 2010), pages 25-42.

4.   Benson P. Shapiro, V. Kasturi Rangan, and John J. Sviokla, "Staple Yourself to an Order," *Harvard Business Review* (July-August, 1992): pages 113-121.

5.   Alice Schroeder, *The Snowball: Warren Buffett and the Business of Life*, (New York: Bantam Dell, 2008).

6.   Adrian J. Slywotzky and David J. Morrison, *The Profit Zone: How Strategic Business Design Will Lead You to Tomorrow's Profits*, (New York: Times Books, a division of Random House, Inc., 1997).

7.   Jane Linder, *Spiral Up (and Other Management Secrets Behind Wildly Successful Initiatives)* (New York: AMACON, 2008).

8.   Daniel H. Pink, *A Whole New Mind* (New York: Riverhead Books, 2006), pages 17-23.

Chapter 6

1.   David A. Price, *The Pixar Touch: The Making of a Company*, (New York: Alfred A. Knopf division of Random House, 2008), page 65.

2.   Margaret Wheatley and Myron Kellner-Rogers. *A Simpler Way* (San Francisco: Berrett-Koehler Publishers, 1999).

3.   Lisa Aschmann, *1000 Songwriting Ideas*, (New York: Hal Leonard Books, 2008).

4.   Clay Shirky, *Cognitive Surplus: Creativity and Generosity in a Connected Age*, (New York: Penguin Press, 2010).

5.   Jane Fulton Suri, *Thoughtless Acts?: Observations on Intuitive Design*, (San Francisco, Chronicle Books, 2007), page 168.

6.   James Webb Young, *A Technique for Producing New Ideas*, (New York, Prosperity Classics from Thinking Ink Media, 2011, original copyright 1942).

7.   Alan Webber, *Rules of Thumb*, (New York: Harper Collins Publishers, 2009), page 242.

Chapter 8

1.   John Kotter and James Heskett, *Corporate Culture and Performance*, (New York: Free Press, 1992), chap. 1.

2.   Andrew Davidson, *1000 CEOs*, (New York: DK Publishers, 2009).

3.   Woody Allen, *Side Effects*, (New York, Ballentine Books, 1986).

4.   Stacy Perman, *In-N-Out Burger: A Behind-the-Counter Look at the Fast-Food Chain that Breaks All the Rules* (New York: Collins Business, 2009).

5.   Edward Tufte, *Beautiful Evidence*, (Cheshire, CT: Graphics Press, 2006).

Chapter 9

1.   Carter Wiseman, *I.M. Pei: A Profile in American Architecture*, (New York: H.N. Abrams, 1990), page 290.

2.   Gordon R. Sullivan and Michael V. Harper, *Hope Is Not a Method* (New York: Times Books, a division of Random House, 1996), page 238.

3D Perspectives

1.   Magic Eye, page 24

2.   View-Master, page 42

3.   Athletes Use 3D Imaging, page 66

4.   3D Express Bus in China, page 96

5.   Google Sketch Up, page 127

6.   Holograms, page 153

7.   3D Printing, page 155

8.   Parametric Modeling, page 174

9.   Uncopyable, page 193

10. 3D Flexibility, page 213

Index

C

228

Customer Effort 17

231

A new dimension
for customers

CUSTOMER

3D™

Bill Self

"What does it truly mean to be customer-centric? Customer 3D ... forces you to look closely
at the realities of your own organization—are you as customer-centered as you thought?"
—Terry Callanan, Chief Quality Officer, Carestream Health Inc.